Be Your B.E.S.T.

Be Your B.E.S.T.

"Only your B.E.S.T. is good enough!"

Dr. Patricia Larkins Hicks

Library of Congress Control Number: 2010907003
ISBN: Hardcover   978-1-4535-0285-3
                 Softcover   978-1-4535-0284-6

This book was printed in the United States of America.

To order additional copies of this book, contact:
Xlibris Corporation
1-888-795-4274
www.Xlibris.com
Orders@Xlibris.com
50311

" . . . faith, hope, and love; the greatest of these is love."

This book is dedicated to my parents who are both deceased
Glover and Herlean Larkins
They gave me the best gift, unconditional love
and
always encouraged and supported me to
Be My Best!

Contents

Acknowledgments

This book was divinely inspired. I give all the honor and glory to God who is the head of my life.

I am especially appreciative of my third grade teacher, Mrs. Beauty Moore, who recognized that I was not performing at my best and did something about it. Because of her intervention, I learned an important lesson that has had a profound impact on my life. Since then, there have been many other teachers to take a similar interest in me being my best. I am grateful for them touching my life as well: Mrs. Josephine Kennedy (deceased), Mrs. Elsie Keyes, Mrs. Nettie Ryan, Dr. Robert Screen, Dr. Bettye Webster (deceased), Dr. G. Albyn Davis, Dr. Daniel S. Beasley, and Dr. Peg Williams.

I am also grateful for the many students, friends, colleagues, and business clients who provided me with the opportunity to learn from our experiences together, many of whom contributed to the key concepts in this book.

There is no task too great or small that can be completed independently. "Be Your B.E.S.T." is the result of the encouragement and feedback of many.

- To Clayton, my husband, who I refer to as my B.E.S.T. buddy and B.E.S.T. man, for his love, support, reminders that kept me on task, and feedback.
- To my extended family for their love and kind gestures of support—Vernanchell Thompson, Keturah Watson, Marian Rivers, and Lucius Black Jr.

- To my adopted brother, Tom Cruse, for his words of encouragement throughout the writing process and editorial feedback.
- To my dear friends and business colleagues—Anne Baird-Bridges, who sat on the beach with me and encouraged me as I developed my book outline; Kathryn Littleton, who I learned the value of analogies and stories and incorporated them into the book format; Celeste Payne, who designed the book cover; Dr. Margaret Roberts (my mentor), who listened, provided guidance, and shared timely advice; Dr. Canise Bean, who provided moments of celebration and lifted my spirit; Audrey Terry, who always checked on me; Karla Smith Fuller, who unselfishly took the time to share; Somers Martin, who supported and helped keep the OMG business projects moving; Nancy Paul, who provided suggestions about how to document my writing experience.
- To my reviewers for taking their personal time to read, share feedback, and provide editorial suggestions—Mechelle Harmon, Shannon Whitfield, and Michael Gordon.

Introduction

You have a purpose for being here. You have been given an assignment that is just for you and special gifts to complete it. However, you do not know the amount of time that you have been allotted to complete your assignment. You are in charge of making it happen and have been given the freedom to choose how you will get it done. So what do you do? How do you make sure you use your gifts and time in a way that will facilitate you completing your assignment? What if you haven't identified your gifts? How do you know when you have made the right choices?

Over the past thirty years, fueled by my passion for results and my work in a variety of workplaces with diverse groups of people, these questions have been asked of me. In the process of assisting others, I have made an important discovery. My discovery is the focus of this book.

> When you are "being your B.E.S.T.," you are able to identify your assignment, develop and use your gifts, make appropriate use of your time and resources, determine the actions you should take, and achieve your desired results. In other words, to complete your assignment on time using what you have been given requires that you *be your B.E.S.T.*

"Being Your B.E.S.T." is about you. No one else can define your B.E.S.T. for you. When you resign your B.E.S.T. to others, you allow them to make choices for you and/or influence your choices. This can result in you doing things that prohibit you from discovering your B.E.S.T., staying in relationships or choosing relationships that prevent you from being your B.E.S.T., obtaining results that are not your B.E.S.T. As you read "Be Your

B.E.S.T.," you will make many discoveries about yourself and the actions that you must take to assist you in making choices that will lead you to your B.E.S.T.

Be Your B.E.S.T. is designed with you in mind. Since we all have stories, I have chosen to tell "my story" as the vehicle for introducing you to what it means to "be your B.E.S.T." Activities associated with my story have been created to connect you with the information from a practical perspective. You can only "be your B.E.S.T." if you use the information to expand on how you view yourself and others. Throughout the book, analogies are used to emphasize key concepts, some of which you will find familiar. These concepts are at the heart of "being your B.E.S.T." In each chapter, you will find "Something to Think About." Questions are raised to stimulate your thinking about how the information presented relates to you. If you are willing to be open, I am certain that you will make some new discoveries about yourself.

"Be" means that you must act. This book is my call to action. It is your guide to self-discoveries that will propel you to "be your B.E.S.T." *B.E.S.T. is not a destination, but rather a journey that will lead you to complete your assignment and achieve your desired results.*

Here are some additional actions that I encourage you to take. *Visit* www.OmgGetsResults.com and review my responses to some of the questions raised in the book. *Share* your story in our *Be Your B.E.S.T. Story Bank*; tell us about the times when you were "being your B.E.S.T." and the results that you achieved. *Join* our *Be Your B.E.S.T. Blog* and let others hear about your discoveries and give you feedback. *Sign up* to receive our *Be Your B.E.S.T. Updates* so that you can receive current information that will assist you in "being your B.E.S.T." *Complete* the *Be Your B.E.S.T. Survey* and let us know what you thought about the book. Your name will be entered in our monthly drawing. You just might win a $25 gift card. If you are on Facebook, *become* a *Be Your B.E.S.T. Fan* and invite your friends to become fans too. Be sure to check out our shopping gallery and select something that will remind you or someone you care about of the importance of "being your B.E.S.T."

Turn now and see why *only your B.E.S.T. is good enough!*

Good Enough

Beware of "good enough,"
It isn't made of sterling stuff;
It's something any person can do,
It marks the many from the few.
It has no merit to the eye,
It's something any person can buy.
Its name is but a sham and bluff,
For it is never "good enough."
With "good enough," the shirkers stop,
In every factory and shop;
With "good enough," the failures rest
And lose to persons who give their best;
With "good enough," the car breaks down
And people fall short of high renown.
Remember and be wise,
In "good enough," disaster lies.
With "good enough" have ships been wrecked,
The forward march of armies checked,
Great buildings burned and fortunes lost;
Nor can the world compute the cost
In life and money it has paid
Because at "good enough" people stayed.
Who stops at "good enough" shall find
Success has left them far behind.
There is no "good enough" that's short
Of what you can do and you ought.
The flaw which may escape the eye
And temporarily get by,
Shall weaken underneath the strain
And wreck the ship or car or train,
For this is true of people and stuff—
Only the B.E.S.T is "good enough."

Original poem
Edgar A. Guest
This is a modification for TEP and societal correctness

Chapter 1

Be Your B.E.S.T.

Learning about "being your B.E.S.T." started for me in the third grade.

~

My Story

I entered kindergarten at age two, was writing my dad letters at four, and started the public school in the second grade. Excelling was my nature. But it was in the third grade that one subject began to give me trouble. In my day, it was called "arithmetic." It didn't come easy to me. In fact, it was a problem. Whenever my teacher mentioned the subject, tears began to fall from my eyes. Deep within dwelled a spirit of fear—fear of failure. As my outbreaks persisted, my teacher, out of concern, gave my mother a call. It was during one of our mother-daughter talks that my mother told me, "Patricia, as long as you are being your best, that is all that matters. Your best may not always result in an 'A' grade." That didn't make sense to me. The best students were recognized by their "A" grades. Now my mother always had a way of teaching me lessons that would prove invaluable to me throughout my life. She helped me to understand that working toward an "A" was the goal. What I needed to do was "be my best." She then helped me to identify some behaviors that would facilitate me "being my best"—listening carefully to my teacher, asking questions when confused or uncertain, completing my homework, doing extra work, preparing for tests, and getting help at home. My parents even got a family friend to come over and work with me on the weekends. Over that school year, I worked hard at "being my best." By the end of the year, my tears had subsided and I was no longer fearful of arithmetic. In fact, it had become one of my favorite subjects, and I had become one of the top students among my peers. Both my teacher and parents were proud of my accomplishment. But it was my mother who reminded me that she was proud of me because *I was "being my best."*

~

My third grade experience taught me that when you are "being your best," you achieve goals, you excel, you stand out, you are satisfied with yourself, and others are satisfied with you. Since this discovery, "being my best" has been a priority of mine, and I have come to understand that *"your best" is a state of being*. This state is guided by your spirit, influenced by your thoughts, and manifested in your behaviors.

- *Being your best* requires *yielding to a spirit* that is greater than your personal will. In everything that you do, it requires putting your faith and trust in a supreme being. You are here on assignment to fulfill a specific mission. Your mission cannot be accomplished if you are not "being your best."
- *Being your best* requires *thinking positive thoughts*. "As a man/woman thinketh so is he/she." How many times have you heard that it is your attitude that determines your altitude? Positive thoughts gain positive outcomes.
- *Being your best* requires *taking action*. You have to get moving and do the things that will make a difference. Sitting idly by and waiting for something to happen is not an option. Getting results depends upon both what you say and what you do.

Over the past thirty years as a result of many additional life lessons, observing and analyzing data about individuals and organizations that have been successful, "best" represents for me the following four key characteristics: *Bright, Excellence, Satisfaction, Timely*. Here is what I now know about *B.E.S.T.*

B = Bright

When you are *Bright*, you are like a star in the night and you shine. You bring light into your space and to the people around you. You stand out. Think about what it is like when you enter a room at night when there is no light. It is difficult for you to find your way. You sometimes bump into obstacles; fumble around, get frustrated and anxious—making it even more difficult to get to your destination. But once you find a light switch, turn it on, and light illuminates the room, it immediately becomes easier to find your way. Did you notice that your fear of falling and frustration diminished? In so many ways, light increases awareness. When you are *Bright*, your antenna is up and you are alert. You are aware of the people and conditions that surround you. You see clearly. You don't miss opportunities because you are able to recognize them. You are able to respond and take action quickly. When you are *Bright*, your ears are open and you hear from a supreme being. You recognize his voice above all others and are not distracted by other voices. When you are *Bright*, you seek to understand before seeking to be understood. Your focus is outward versus inward; it is not about me, but rather it is about others. You understand what is being communicated to you by others. When you are *Bright*, you are hopeful and positive. As such you do not set limitations and boundaries. You view the glass as "half-full" versus "half empty." The possibilities are endless. A "half-full" view causes you to continue on in search of solutions. When you are *Bright*, you are joyful and a joy to be around. You encourage and support; you lift others up. When you are *Bright*, you let your light shine; your inner glow guides you to your highest good—to "be your *B*.e.s.t."

E = Excellence

When you *Ex*cel, a standard is established. Your aim is the stars. You recognize that the place where you are today can always be better. There is more—bigger, better, "best!" When you are *Ex*cellent, you take ownership. You blaze the trail. You create the path that others follow. You believe there is no limit to what can be accomplished. When you are *Ex*cellent, you are prepared for the task or situation at hand. You do what is necessary. You make sure that the details have been attended to and that what you do is accurate, complete, and appropriate. When you strive for *Ex*cellence, you continue to stretch and extend yourself. You let nothing or no one stop you. Obstacles are to be overcome. Barriers are to be broken. Opportunities abound. You look forward with anticipation and operate at full throttle—you give everything you do your all. Your goal is simply to "be your B.*E*.s.t."

S = Satisfaction

When you are *S*atisfied with yourself and others are satisfied too, there is peace and harmony; a sense of contentment overcomes you. You feel fulfilled. You are happy and can't help but smile. *Satisfaction* means that your mind, body, and spirit are in alignment. When you are *Satisfied*, you have a positive sense of self and are confident. You know what you are capable of doing. You know what you need to do. You know what it will take for you to do it. You just do it! *Satisfaction* results in expressions of gratitude and appreciation. Needs and expectations are met, both yours and those you touch. *Satisfaction* means that you bless others, and blessings multiply. This state of being energizes you to continue striving to "be your B.E.*S*.t."

T = *Timely*

When you are *Timely*, you count every minute and you make every minute count. You recognize the value of time. You know that once time is used you cannot reclaim it. That time is gone. You also recognize that you really don't know how much time is available to you to accomplish your life's mission. Hence, you spend your time wisely. When you are *Timely*, you think about what you do. You choose wisely. Yet you balance how you spend your time. Remember, "there is a time for work and a time to play." You spend time taking care of self because your mental, physical, and spiritual state influences what you achieve. When you are *Timely*, you recognize that achieving and succeeding is about others. Therefore, you make sure that you spend time cultivating and maintaining relationships. A key driver to "being your best" is tied to the type and quality of relationships that are a part of your life. When you are *Timely*, you respect others' time. You are on time. Your timing is right. You are prompt. You are in step with the universe. Managing your time wisely assists you "being your B.E.S. *T*."

Simply speaking, being your B.E.S.T. brings moments that you . . .
find enjoyment, achieve goals, live to the fullest, and succeed!

Accomplishing your life's mission requires that you must "be your B.E.S.T."

Being My B.E.S.T Activity

1. Think about a time in your life when you were "being your B.E.S.T."

I was being my B.E.S.T. when . . .

2. Review the B.E.S.T. descriptions. Given the situation that you identified above, describe your personal B.E.S.T.

My Personal B.E.S.T.

B.

E.

S.

T.

Here's My Example . . .

I was being my B.E.S.T. when I interviewed for a position with my national professional association.

My Personal B.E.S.T. Interview

B. I prepared for the interview by gathering as much information as I could about the organization including its culture, people, and focus. This knowledge allowed me to be *B*right-I dressed professionally, greeted everyone with a smile and firm handshake, and entered the interview with a sense of confidence.

E. During the interview, I demonstrated my *E*xcellence. Through my responses the persons interviewing me could see that I was prepared and had the skills needed for the position. When appropriate, I restated and paraphrased their questions, provided cogent responses and navigated to the heart of the questions asked.

S. Through their feedback, I recognized that the interviewers were *S*atisfied with me. As such, I became more relaxed and comfortable. My personal level of *S*atisfaction increased and so did my confidence. The interview began to feel as if we were engaged in a stimulating conversation that was being enjoyed by all participants.

T. I was on *T*ime. Arriving fifteen minutes early gave me an opportunity to get a sense of the work environment, settle myself, and reduce my interview jitters. By the time I heard my name called, I was prepared to start my interview at the established time.

So how do you *really* know when you are "being your B.E.S.T.?"

What does "being your B.E.S.T." look like?

In the previous activity, we both made assumptions about our B.E.S.T. We described what we thought was our B.E.S.T. Can we be certain that our descriptions are accurate? Do they indeed reflect our B.E.S.T.? Were there factors that influenced us being our B.E.S.T. that we did not recognize?

Given we each are unique and have been given different gifts and missions, then B.E.S.T. is not the same for everyone. *Knowing your B.E.S.T.* requires engaging in an action that provides you with the right information about your personal B.E.S.T. This required action is one that most of us ignore or have not fully integrated in a conscious way into our daily activities. To "be your B.E.S.T." requires that you *measure.*

- Measuring involves ongoing tracking, counting, analyzing, and interpreting of information
- Measuring allows you to define and confirm for yourself what is B.E.S.T.
- Measuring helps you to know yourself
- Measuring facilitates growth and improvement

We all have had minimal experience measuring our B.E.S.T. Rather, we have allowed others to measure us repeatedly and tell us from their measures what is our B.E.S.T. from their perspective. We have allowed others to define for us when we are "being our B.E.S.T." Think about all the situations that you have depended upon someone else to measure your B.E.S.T. At school, teachers measured to determine your best using a variety of measures. Some of the measures used were designed by them while other measures were designed by individuals who were not familiar with you. While enrolled in school, how many times did you measure to determine your personal B.E.S.T.? Think about your health status. How many times have you relied upon the doctor and/or nurse to measure and tell you about your weight, blood pressure, glucose level? Think about your workplace. How many times have you tracked your productivity without being asked to do so by your supervisor? There are countless situations which can be identified that others have been relied upon to measure us. Additionally, others have been given the latitude to select the suitable tools, analyze the results, and make the correct interpretation. In many instances, the results reported and interpreted to us by others did not reflect our thoughts nor represented what we wanted to hear. In turn, many of us have developed a dislike for measures and measurement.

Over the past thirty years, the little girl who cried when she heard arithmetic has made many meaningful discoveries about numbers. They tell a story, much like words. Measurement has personal value; without it, optimal results cannot be achieved. In fact, my adopted mantra is "that which gets measured gets managed." "Being your B.E.S.T." requires that measures are tied to gathering information about your spirit, attitudes, and behaviors on a regular basis. Also, there are factors that impact you "being our B.E.S.T.," and these must be measured as well. When you measure, it is essential that appropriate methods, tools are used and measurement occurs at appropriate intervals of time. More importantly, after measuring it is incumbent upon you to do something with the information. It is necessary to find meaning from the data collected, use it in decision making, and determining a course of action. My greatest discovery is that to "be your B.E.S.T." requires personal measurement.

When you do not measure, you are at risk for not "being your B.E.S.T.";
in fact, you have relinquished determining your B.E.S.T.
to someone other than yourself.
To "be your B.E.S.T." and know it requires that, you must measure.

Something to Think About . . .

- Do you collect information about your spirit, attitudes, and behaviors on a regular basis?

    [ ] Yes [ ] No [ ] Somewhat

- Do you know what factors impact you "being your B.E.S.T.?"
  [ ] Yes [ ] No [ ] Somewhat

- Do you measure these factors frequently?
  [ ] Yes [ ] No [ ] Sometimes

- Do you know if you are using appropriate measurement methods and tools?
  [ ] Yes [ ] No [ ] Somewhat

- Have you used information that you collected about yourself to define when you are "being your B.E.S.T.?"
  [ ] Yes [ ] No [ ] Sometimes

If you answered "No" or "Somewhat/Sometimes" to any of these questions, this book is for you. *Over the next chapters you will learn more about how to determine when you are "being your B.E.S.T." This book introduces the measurement basics in a practical way. The tips provided will assist you in making measurement a part of your daily activities. In fact, measurement will become one of your B.E.S.T. practices.*

If you answered "Yes" to all of the questions, keep reading. *You are certain to find some new information that will assist you in knowing you are "being your B.E.S.T." As you explore the chapters in this book, you will find confirmation that you are doing what it takes to "be your B.E.S.T."*

Remember: *To "be your B.E.S.T.," changes over your lifetime as you grow, develop, and change.*

Chapter 2

Embrace Your B.E.S.T. Practice

"Being your B.E.S.T." so that you are in control of your destiny and can accomplish your life's mission necessitates that you adopt as your B.E.S.T. practice measurement. Measurement is a B.E.S.T. practice because it is an essential fact-finding process that gathers information needed to make informed choices. Life is all about choices. There is a direct link between your choices and the path your life takes. Choices determine your attitude. Ultimately, your choices determine whether goals are achieved and life's assignment is completed. In the absence of measurement, assumptions are made or guesses about your B.E.S.T., and others have been granted the opportunity to take charge of your life and determine your B.E.S.T. Embracing measurement as a B.E.S.T. practice requires understanding the measurement basics, developing a few basic skills, and making these skills daily habits. Let's get started by examining first the basics.

Measurement Basics

While measurement is a complex process that sometimes can be daunting, the purpose of this section is to introduce you to three basic yet essential facts about measurement. They represent the fundamentals that you must understand in order to make measurement a B.E.S.T. practice.

1. **Measurement is a discovery process**. Think of measurement as an inquisitive course of action. At the center is a key component—inquiry. This process involves exploration, examination, and investigation.

Do you remember the childhood game, "hide-and-seek?" This simple game included people hiding, or someone hiding an item from you. The goal was for you to find the people hiding or the hidden item. As you looked, you were actually involved in a discovery process; you were measuring.

Something to Think About . . .

- Did you enjoy playing the game? Was it fun?
- Were you thoughtful about how you went about looking or did you just look randomly?
- Did you recognize the connection between how you looked and achieving the goal?
- Were some participants more successful than others in achieving the goal? Was it that they were luckier or had they maybe unknowingly embarked upon the discovery process?

Let's see what your responses reveal about your readiness to embrace measurement as a B.E.S.T. practice.

- If you enjoyed hide-and-seek and found it fun, you will recognize more easily the benefit of measuring. If the game was not fun to you, keep reading because throughout the book you will uncover multiple examples that ultimately will convince you measurement is a B.E.S.T. practice that is essential if you are to reach your goals; in fact, it will help you clarify and determine your goals.
- If you took time before you began looking to consider what clues might assist you in your hunt, you will engage more quickly in activities that will support your guesses or premises. If you started looking without considering clues, keep reading because you will discover that there are always clues and missing them can cost you time and may prevent you from being your B.E.S.T.
- If you connected how you looked to finding the person or item, you will more readily appreciate the relationship between processes

and outcomes. If you don't see or believe there is a relationship between processes and outcomes, keep reading so that you can gain insight into this relationship and how it ultimately impacts you being your B.E.S.T.

- If you believe that luck is not a determinant of success, you will more readily recognize that your success is tied to your actions. If you depend upon luck or think that luck in some way influences success, keep reading so that you can once and for all understand that nothing in life happens by chance.

When you engage in the discovery process, the status in quo is rejected; instead there is a quest for improvement, innovation, and breakthrough. Having an inquiring mind and being willing to explore and investigate is critical to "being your B.E.S.T."

2. **Measurement involves gathering the right information (data) or signs (evidence).** Collecting the right information assists you in making accurate and precise choices and/or decisions. Don't assume you know because more often than not there is more to know than you realize. Given that change is today's constant, it is incumbent upon you to be vigilant in your search for accurate and complete information. Determining that you are collecting the right information requires doing some homework or research. A few years ago, I decided to lose weight. There were several signs that led me to this decision. One sign was tied to my inability to go to a significant event of one of my dearest friends. In fact, this was the first major event in her life that I had missed; it was her daughter's wedding. I was all packed and ready to go, when all of a sudden I felt this excruciating pain in my legs. There was so much pain that it was difficult for me to walk, much less drive. Instead of being at the church, I found myself in the hospital getting an x-ray. The doctor used the term "osteoarthritis." This was a familiar problem because my mother had suffered from the same condition. Her doctor had attributed it to aging, and now so was my doctor. However, after gathering information from other medical references,

it was revealed that next to aging, obesity is the most powerful risk factor for osteoarthritis of the knees. Taking that information, coupled with the fact that I was now buying clothes two sizes larger than my normal dress size, the decision was clear to me that losing weight was no longer an option; it was a necessity. Gathering accepted information about osteoarthritis coupled with my personal information helped me to make an informed and accurate decision that has aided me in "being my B.E.S.T."

Something to Think About . . .

- Identify a decision that you made recently.
- What information did you use to assist you in your decision?
- Was it the precise information that you needed?
- What was the source of your information?
- Were there other sources that you could have utilized too?

Too often, decisions are made with either limited information or inaccurate information. Measurement requires that you think about the information that is needed to make an informed decision.

3. **Appropriate tools are necessary to assist in collecting the right information.** Not just any tool will do. In fact, the wrong tool will lead to gathering incomplete and/or inaccurate information, wasting time and resources, making the wrong conclusion and/or decision. It is imperative that the right tool is selected; in fact, sometimes multiple tools are needed.

In the personal example of losing weight, there are a variety of tools that might be used to measure weight loss. My first selection of a tool focused on a scale that would provide information about my body weight. Upon arriving at the store, there were many scales to choose from and upon reviewing the product descriptions it became apparent that several of them provided different information. To select the appropriate tool required more homework on my part. First, it was necessary to determine the right information that needed to be collected that would determine weight loss. After gathering data about weight loss from articles, books, and health care professionals, it was now easier for me to determine the information that needed to be collected. My decision was to focus on body weight, body fat composition, body mass index, and body hydration. The next step was to determine which scales collected this information. Four scales were found. Aside from looking at what information the scale provided, I decided on a number of additional factors, including cost, ease of use, size, reliability, data storage. A comparison was made across the four scales of the aforementioned factors. Also, it helped me to read the reviews of users, especially the reviewers that were my age and gender. Using the information gathered and comparative analysis, my decision was made. I felt that the right tool to measure the right information had been chosen. But was this the only tool that I needed? Remember the earlier reference to the relationship between process and outcomes. Let's examine that relationship here. In order to lose weight, there were two other areas from my research that appeared important for me to gather information; these included physical activity and caloric intake. Given my sedentary lifestyle, tracking the number of steps taken daily led me to examining pedometers. My daily use of the Internet led me to an on-line calorie calculator. There is no away around it, selecting the right tools require that you do some research. This includes identifying the available tools, data that can be gathered using the tool, and usefulness of the tool as it relates to you personally.

Something to Think About . . .

- How will you determine what information you will need to make an informed decision?
- What will you do to ensure you have identified all the tools that will provide you with the information you need?
- What personal characteristics do you want to make sure you consider when you select a tool?

Making sure the right tools are being used when measuring is absolutely a must to ensure you are gathering the right information. Remember, informed choices assist you in "being your B.E.S.T."

Measurement is not an alternative. It is the "B.E.S.T. practice" that you must embrace if you want to "be your B.E.S.T."

Measurement Basic Skills

Let's turn now to examining the following three primary skills needed to engage in the B.E.S.T. practice measurement.

- **Observation:** This skill requires that you keep your eyes and ears open to absorb everything that comes your way. Information is sent to you constantly, in a variety of forms. Whether you receive the information and make sense from it depend upon your observation skills. Remember the saying, "You can't see the forest for the trees." Sometimes you can be so focused on your personal goals, actions, needs, and interests that you miss the key information that could in fact help you achieve your goals, improve your actions, clarify your needs and interests. In other words, it is difficult to be your B.E.S.T. if you are not observing what is around you, learning from your observations, and more importantly putting your observations to use. Take my personal example. In the morning on my way to work, I spent my time rushing out the door focused on the day ahead: meetings, projects, tasks, and timelines. My attention was directed totally toward my plan for the day ahead. One morning, a friend picked me up for work. A bird was chirping. The friend asked if I had heard the sound. "What sound?" I asked. My friend replied, "The bird chirping—it's a sign that spring is near." At that moment pausing to observe the bird's sound, I wondered how long I had been missing that bird. This situation heighted my awareness that a trait such as "focus" could also prohibit you from identifying valuable information.

Now this example also provides two illustrations. The first focuses on observation—hearing and recognizing the bird's sound. The second illustration focuses on the interpretation that is made from the observation, "spring is near." You must be mindful that the interpretation of what you observe is shaped by your culture, experiences, and previous knowledge. Hence, two people can make the same observations but have different interpretations. Enhancing your observation skills requires that you keep your eyes and ears open at all times and you seek continually to understand that which you observe. To be your B.E.S.T. demands that you develop the skill of observation and use it daily.

Practice: The following are suggestions to assist you in developing your observation skills. Also, take an observation skills test so that you can determine how observant you are. Your test results will provide an indication of how much practice you will need in sharpening your observation skills.

1. During daily tasks keep your eyes and ears open to your surroundings.
2. People watch and make note of your observations.
3. Take different routes and observe your surroundings.
4. Identify three items of information that you will take from a meeting that will help you be more effective, complete your work, or build better relationships with people attending the meeting.
5. Try something new (for example, food item, radio station, exercise, etc.) and use your senses to identify how you are impacted.

• **Active listening:** This skill requires that you hold judgment so that you can hear and understand the total message being communicated. Listening actively involves paying careful attention to the other person who is communicating. This can be difficult because sometimes you allow your mind to day dream, be distracted, or think about the key messages you want to communicate. In other words, you lose focus on what the other person is saying. Politicians appear to be notorious for not listening actively. How many times have you observed a politician when asked a question to respond repeatedly with remarks that appear to be prepared? No wonder it is difficult to find common ground; more often than not politicians seek to share versus understand.

Your personal filters, assumptions, judgments, and beliefs can alter what you hear. It is essential then that you clarify what you have heard. To do this, you will need to summarize what you think you heard, ask questions to verify your understanding, and/or paraphrase what was said. Let's examine another personal example. I was planning a retreat with two colleagues. We were meeting the week before the retreat to finalize our plans. One of the colleagues said we might need to reconsider the date of the retreat. I responded that everyone had it on their calendars and was expecting us to have the retreat. The other colleague indicated that participants would not think we were serious if we changed the date at this late hour. Many of the participants in fact had already altered plans to make the current date. We agreed to go forth. Was that the right decision? Had we listened to understand or were we guilty of focusing on sharing our point of view? Listening to understand, we could have said, "Has something come up that no longer makes this a good date for you?" or "Sounds like there's something that may make this date not work for you anymore." Depending upon our colleague's response, we may have made a different decision.

Listening actively is an important skill that will assist you in gathering the right information so that you can make the correct decision and "be your B.E.S.T."

Practice: The following are suggestions to assist you in practicing developing your active listening skills. Listening is one aspect of communication that we have been the least prepared. Very few of us have had courses in listening. To determine how effective you are at listening, you should take an active listening test. Your results will indicate the extent to which you may need to develop your listening skills.

1. When someone is speaking, put aside distracting thoughts. Don't daydream, and don't develop your rebuttal.

2. When someone is speaking, tune out environmental factors (for example, noises, people talking, room temperature, etc.) that can be distracting and stay focused on the speaker.

3. When someone is speaking to you, pay attention to their body language and determine what messages are being communicated nonverbally. Remember to verify your assumptions.

4. When someone is speaking to you, allow the speaker to finish. Don't interrupt.

5. Before ending the conversation, summarize your understanding to make sure you and the speaker are leaving on the same page.

- **Asking questions:** The skill of asking the right question is at the core of measurement. While questions come in a variety of forms, for the purpose of this B.E.S.T. practice, the following three are most important—closed, open, and probing. Understanding each question form is helpful in determining when it is most appropriate to be used. A single word or very short factual answer is usually elicited from a *closed question*. Additionally, a closed question seeks information to test your understanding, or the other person's, concludes a discussion, or makes a decision. For example, "Where did you go to elementary school?" "Are you hungry?" "Now that we have heard from everyone, are we ready to close discussion?" On the other hand, *open questions* elicit longer responses and seek to gather information about the respondent's knowledge, opinions, or feelings. For example, "Tell me how you think the president is doing?" "What do you think about the new taxes?" "How was your vacation?" One caution to be mindful of is when asking an open question that begins with "why." A "why" question appears to be evaluative. For example, "Why were you late?" The person responding may become defensive and spend more time justifying being late rather than sharing pertinent information about the factors that contributed to being late. *Probing questions* are used to gain clarification or draw out more information from people who are trying to avoid telling you something. Probing questions elicit details.

For example, "What exactly do you mean about patient-centered care?" "Who attended the meeting?"

Aside from asking the right questions to ensure that you gather the right information, consider your tone of voice, body language, location, and timing. All of these factors influence the information you receive. Embracing measurement as your B.E.S.T. practice involves learning how, when, and what questions to ask.

Practice: The following are suggestions to assist you in developing appropriate questions.

1. Ask a closed question in a group situation that will assist the group in making a decision.
2. Ask a closed question that tests your understanding.
3. Ask an open question that will assist you in getting more details.
4. Ask an open question that will assist you in understanding other's knowledge.
5. Ask a probing question that will assist you in gaining clarification to ensure you understand the whole story.

Making Measurement a Habit

To be your B.E.S.T. requires that you know where you are with regard to the four B.E.S.T. characteristics. You can only know your B.E.S.T. by measuring; otherwise you are guessing or making assumptions. It is important that you integrate this B.E.S.T. practice into your daily routine. Make it a habit much like brushing your teeth. As such, you will retain control of your destiny. The following are six steps to follow that will assist you in making measurement a habit.

1. **Commit to measuring over a twenty-one-day period.** That is, how long it is estimated it will take to ensure that this B.E.S.T. practice becomes a habit. Scientifically, it has been proven that if

you perform a new daily habit every single day for twenty-one days, chances are you will keep it. Share your commitment with a person in your life space who will check on you to make sure you are on course. This person can be your B.E.S.T. buddy. Make sure you start with a realistic twenty-one-day time period. In other words, if you are going on vacation, starting a new job, preparing for an exam, this is not a good time to begin integrating measurement into your daily routine.

2. **Use the B.E.S.T. daily tracking log.** Be accountable to yourself by tracking daily your progress. Documenting what you do will provide you with tangible evidence that shows you did it.

3. **Conduct a B.E.S.T. checkup at the start of your day, midday, and the end of the day.** Establish this checkup if possible as part of another daily routine. For example, during a meal, workout, meditation period, etc. Ask yourself a closed question that lets you know the status of the four B.E.S.T. characteristics.

4. **Keep your ears and eyes open; draw upon your senses throughout the day to determine what factors are impacting you being your B.E.S.T.** Reflect upon your day; this can be at the end of the day or the beginning of the next day. Using the B.E.S.T. daily tracking log, jot down the factors that influenced you "being your B.E.S.T." and those that got in the way and prevented you from "being your B.E.S.T."

5. **Assess your use of the fundamental skills.** Reflect upon your day; this can be at the end of the day or the beginning of the next day. Identify the skills you used over the course of the day and the level of effectiveness. Determine to what extent you were able to gather the right information to assist you at "being your B.E.S.T."

6. **Identify what you must measure to ensure you are at your B.E.S.T.** Tomorrow is a new day. Given what you uncovered about today, decide what you must keep track of the next day to ensure you are "being your B.E.S.T." You can make this decision at the end of the day or at the beginning of the next day.

Repeat these six steps each day over the next twenty-one days. Share your results so that others can be encouraged. Send your story and B.E.S.T. tracking Log to www.OmgGetsResults.com

Points to Remember

- **Every day it is necessary to collect data about the four characteristics that define your personal B.E.S.T.** On a daily basis, you need to engage in gathering information (data) or signs (evidence) that will indicate that you are being your B.E.S.T.

- **Collecting the right information is vital to assisting you in determining your B.E.S.T.** Make sure you have identified what information you need to collect. The right information may be influenced by when you collect it (timing) and where you collect it (location).

- **You may need to do some research to ensure that you have identified correctly what information you need to collect.** Given change is constant, there is always something new to learn. Also recognize that sometimes you have preconceived ideas (bias) and don't realize it. Your bias can influence your judgment.

- **Information needs to be collected using the appropriate tools.** Make sure you select tools that will provide you with the information you have identified that you need. Also make sure you review the description of the tool and that it meets your criteria for usefulness. There are many tools available that can shed light about the four B.E.S.T. characteristics. Collecting information from a variety of tools will help you verify that you have come to the correct conclusion.

- **You are integral to this B.E.S.T. practice.** Make sure that you continually work to develop the fundamental skills and integrate these into your day. Only you can ensure that measurement becomes your B.E.S.T. practice.

What will you do with this information to "be your B.E.S.T."?

Chapter 3

Understand Your B.E.S.T. Context

A key factor that influences you "being your B.E.S.T." is your *context.* Simply put, context is your environment, and it contains both physical surroundings and people. Your environment plays an integral role in providing the stimuli necessary for "being your B.E.S.T." *Daily these two variables, physical surroundings and people, influence how you think and act.*

Let's return to my story and find out about the context.

~

My Story

The community I grew up in was small, a population of about fifty-five thousand people. The pace was slow, the sun was my alarm clock, and the skies were blue most of the time. It seemed like a tropical resort because there were palm trees, boats, tourists, and lots of water. In fact, a river separated the mainland from the beach side. Going to the beach was my favorite activity. I enjoyed hearing the roaring sounds of the ocean waves, feeling the sun's rays beaming down on me, watching the seagulls take flight. Being on the beach and soaking in the sun made me feel alert and energized.

My dad was the provider for the family and worked long hours as a chef at one of the major hotels on the beach. Sometimes on his way to work, he took me to school. Riding with my dad was fun. All the way to school we engaged in conversation, and he never tired listening. I came to recognize that patience was one of his virtues. Almost every time en route to my school, my godfather could be seen sweeping the steps of "The Little Gypsy Tearoom," a place that he and my godmother owned. It was the only fancy place you could go out to eat in the neighborhood. And there were sleeping rooms that people could rent if they needed somewhere to stay while visiting the area. When we approached "The Little Gypsy Tearoom," it signaled that we were approaching my school, which was about two blocks away.

South Street Elementary School, named after the street it was located, had a family-like culture. Whether it was the cafeteria worker who wanted to make sure you had a tasty lunch that you ate, or the custodian who made sure the school was clean and comfortable for you, or the safety patrol director who welcomed you upon arrival and made sure you crossed the street safely, you always felt everyone working at the school was looking out for you and you were important to them.

Everyone in my class was greeted with a warm smile from our teacher. She showed her students that they were loved, each in her own special way. It was not unusual to see our principal walking by the classroom. Everyone knew the school leader; just her presence communicated she was in charge and expected you to excel. No one wanted to be singled out by the principal unless it was for having done something well.

Parents were intimately involved in the school, and mine were no exception. In fact, my mother was no stranger to everyone at school. She always attended the PTA meetings and could be counted on to help out on our school trips. She was a homemaker and managed everything and everyone with precision and attention to detail, including me.

Every day after arriving home from school, my mother would have a snack waiting for me. While I snacked, it was her time to find out about my day. She could be counted on to ask me at least four questions—"How was your day?" "What did you do in school?" "What did you learn today?" "Do you have any homework?" My mother always had time for me and displayed an interest in what I was learning and doing. After my snack, it was time to visit my grandmother who lived down the street in the house at the next corner. It only took a few minutes for me to walk to her house. She greeted me with a hug and always appeared eager to hear my daily stories. Because she was such an attentive listener and edged me on, I would light up like a Christmas tree and become animated as I shared my daily adventures. It became apparent to me later in life that I was her afternoon entertainment.

You see, everyone loved having me around because my parents had been waiting a long time for my arrival. Prior to my birth, my parents had been married twenty-five years and lived in the same neighborhood. They knew everyone. The neighborhood was comprised of eight houses, a church, and community store. In fact, my house was adjacent to the community store and directly across the street from the church. Because of its location, I got to see and know most of the people who came and left my neighborhood.

For me, the neighborhood seemed like a large family that was comprised of family members living in different houses on the same street. I even had big sisters and brothers, because over the years my parents had taken care of other children in the neighborhood, many of whom were now in high school or finishing college. In fact, my big brother would periodically check my homework when he came to visit. I loved showing him my homework. We would review it at my desk. My desk at home was much larger than the one at school. There were lots of drawers for me to store my paper and other school supplies. Even at night, I enjoyed working at my desk because there was a special lamp that I could turn on to do my reading. My dad would often have to remind me to turn it off before I went to bed.

It was my parents' experiences with children in the neighborhood that made them both committed to making sure I was loved but not spoiled. My parents only wanted for me to "be my B.E.S.T."

Your environment forms a context that shapes and influences your thoughts and actions. In fact, research indicates that attitudes are shaped as early as five years of age. You may not realize that much of what you think and do today is influenced by the location where you grew up as a child and the people who spent time with you during your childhood. There are many attributes of your physical surroundings that impact you. Some of these include its size, space, pace, climate, region, culture, resources. Similarly, the values, attitudes, interests, experiences, knowledge, aspirations, preferences of the people around you play an integral role in shaping your personal values, attitudes, aspirations, interests, knowledge, and preferences. This profound influence is the reason you have been reminded throughout life to be selective of the people you associate with and bring into your life space.

Something to Think About . . .

- Where did you grow up?
- Who inspired you when you were a child?
- When you think about your childhood physical surroundings, what attributes come to mind?
- Can you remember being reminded to be careful in selecting your friends because they may influence your behavior? Who reminded you?
- How did your childhood friends influence your thoughts and actions? Who else influenced your thinking and actions?

It is vital that you understand how being your B.E.S.T. is impacted by your physical surroundings and people around you. When you don't know or understand the influencing and shaping that is occurring in your environment, you make choices that hinder you from "being your B.E.S.T." and what is more important—you don't recognize it at the time. Had you known, you would have been able to make more informed decisions. Lack of understanding about the effect of your physical surroundings and people around you can result in working and living in places that hinder you from being as productive and successful as you could be, forming and staying in relationships that prevent you from doing the things that make you happy, healthy, and prosperous. On the other hand, *early identification of the effect of your environment including its physical surroundings and people can assist you in being in the right place with the right people so that you can "be your B.E.S.T."*

Here's My Example

Based upon my story, think about my context, both the physical surroundings and people around me. Identify eight attributes of my physical surroundings and people that you think impacted me "being my B.E.S.T."

Physical Surroundings Attributes	People
1.	1.
2.	2.
3.	3.
4.	4.
5.	5.
6.	6.
7.	7.
8.	8.

As you identified these attributes and people, did you realize that there were different locations within my physical surroundings? These included my home, school, neighborhood, and community. In a subsequent chapter, the interconnectedness of these locations will be further explored. For now, here are some examples of the attributes that have been identified from my physical surroundings. As you review the examples, think about which specific location they represent.

Attributes of My Physical Surroundings: slow pace, sunshine, school climate, prepared snack, family car, small population, tourism, church

People Around Me: Dad, Mother, school staff, Grandmother, Godparents, tourists, principal, neighbors

Something to Think About . . .

- What attributes did you associate with my home, school, neighborhood, and community?
- What people did you identify that were in my home, school neighborhood, and community?

At Your B.E.S.T. Activity

> **Refer back to the discussion about context. Now think about the physical surroundings that formed your childhood context. What different locations made up your surroundings? List them here.**

Now choose one of the locations in your childhood physical surroundings and identify at least four attributes and four people that influenced and shaped you.

Physical Surroundings Attributes   **People**

1.   1.

2.   2.

3.   3.

4.   4.

Since each *location* has many attributes and people that can impact you "being your B.E.S.T.," how do you know which ones are significant? Without measuring you can't really know. At this point, the attributes and people that have been identified in this activity reflect only our assumptions. It is incredible how frequently we act based upon a guess, conjecture, and supposition. Sometimes assumptions are accurate, while other times they are proven to be incorrect. Verifying assumptions is critical because it can prevent you from wasting time, making costly mistakes, engaging in conflict, missing opportunities, and attaining your goals. In other words if you want to make the optimal use of your time, stay focused, seize opportunities, and achieve, you must act based upon verification of assumptions. You must utilize your B.E.S.T. practice measurement.

Let us see what you can discover about your B.E.S.T. by putting into practice the information shared in the previous chapter about measurement and connecting what you now know about context to the four characteristics of B.E.S.T. as introduced in the first chapter. The following activity is designed to assist you in analyzing the context of my story and its impact on me "being my B.E.S.T."

Contextual Analysis

Review *My Story* in this chapter and look for the signs and clues. Use the Discovering My Context table to assist you in your discovery. Think about each of the four B.E.S.T. characteristics and identify the attributes of my physical environment and people that you think influenced me "being my B.E.S.T." Indicate what clue or sign you used to select the attribute and person.

Discovering My Context

B.E.S.T. Characteristics	Physical Surroundings Attribute	Clue	People	Clue
Bright—aware and alert; stand out				
Excellent— setting the standard				
Satisfaction— content with self and other's content with you				
Timely—on time				

Go to www.OMGGetsResults.com and compare your responses to mine.

How do you know the attributes that you identified really impacted me "being my B.E.S.T.?" To really know, it requires that you measure to verify. Let's put into practice what you read in chapter two.

Looking at your table, did you identify the sun as an attribute in my physical surroundings that might impact me being *Timely*? Was the clue that you used to identify this attribute *"the sun was like an alarm clock?"* Given this clue, you need to know more about my opinion. You might use an open-ended question to uncover this additional information.

Open Question: What is it about the sun that makes you see it as an alarm clock?

My Response: When the sun comes up, I don't need my alarm clock because my body awakes from the rays of the sun.

Open Question: What happens on a day when there is no sunlight?

My Response: I need my alarm clock because I won't automatically wake up.

Now that you have more clarification, it is time to put your observation skills to work. In other words, what might you observe to gather data about this relationship?

Observation: You could observe the time I awoke without an alarm clock, both when the sun is shining and when it is not.

There are key variables that influence the attributes of our physical surroundings. These include: location, space, size, climate, pace, resources, and terrain. It is important that you consider these variables as you measure. In this example, you are examining the relationship of the sun to my awakening. Given the variables identified, it appears that *location* would be a key influencer regarding the sun. In other words, *where the sun is located* when it rises is important to know because *its location would play a key role in the sun's ability to impact me.*

Upon careful review of your table, you will note that the sun is an attribute that may impact other B.E.S.T. characteristics, *Bright* and *Satisfaction*. This one attribute may be significant if it is found to influence multiple aspects of me being my *B.E.S.T.* This example suggests that some contextual variables may be more significant than others, because they impact multiple characteristics of your B.E.S.T. Hence, it is important that when you gather data about the attributes of your physical surroundings, you remember to examine if the attribute is impacting more than one B.E.S.T. characteristic; you consider the significance of the attribute. We will examine significance again in a subsequent chapter.

Something to Think About . . .

Now reexamine your table. Select another attribute of my physical surroundings that you identified.

- What attribute did you identify as impacting me being satisfied?
- What clue led you to your selection?
- What question(s) will you ask to verify that your choice is correct?
- What observation(s) will you make to confirm your assumption?

Go to www.OMGGetsResults.com to see my example.

Turn now to examine the people who may have impacted me "being my B.E.S.T." Return to your table again. Did you identify my mother as a person that impacted me being *Excellent*?

Was the clue that you used to identify this attribute *"She could be counted on to ask me at least four questions—How was your day? What did you do in school? What did you learn today? Did you do your homework?"* Given this clue, you need to know more about what my mother did with the information I shared. You might use a probing question to obtain additional details.

Probing Question: When you asked Patricia "What did you learn today," How did you handle her responses?

My Mother's Response: If she said "nothing," then I would find ways to get Patricia to think about her day and recognize that she did learn something.

If she said she learned to read a story in her book, then I would ask Patricia to read it for me.

I would always encourage her by telling her how proud I was of her.

Having more clarification, it is time now to put your observation skills to work again. In other words, what might you observe to gather data about my mother's impact on me being excellent? It is difficult to gather information about relationships from direct observation. You don't know how the people engaged in the interaction perceive the impact of the interaction. Perhaps that is why you are unable to readily recognize the impact people in your life space have on you being your B.E.S.T. Instead of direct observation, you can examine the impact of relationships by gathering indirect evidences. For example, you could ask me an open-ended question to gather my opinion.

Open Question: Who in your family has influenced you the most to excel?

My Response: My mother was probably the most influential person.

Open Question: What was it about your mother that encouraged you to excel?

My Response: She always encouraged me and made me feel that I could do anything. And with that encouragement was always the reminder to "be my best."

There are key variables that influence the impact people have in our lives. These include their attitudes, behaviors, and interests. It is important that you consider these as you measure their personal impact. In this example, it appears that the behaviors and interests of my mother are key influencers. In other words, my mother's questions asked daily after school coupled with her direct interest in my performance in school contributed to her impact on me "being my B.E.S.T."

As you review your table, you probably identified my mother as a person that may impact all of the B.E.S.T. characteristics. Hence, you might assume that she is one person in my life who played a significant role in shaping and influencing me to "be my *B.E.S.T.*"

Gathering information about your physical surroundings and the people in your life space helps to clarify the physical attributes and people that are influencing and shaping your B.E.S.T. characteristics. This is an important first step to understand how your context influences you "being your B.E.S.T." The next step is necessary if you are to "be your B.E.S.T." This step involves gaining meaning from the information gathered and using it to aid you in making informed choices—data-driven decisions.

My Contextual Data-Driven Decisions

The following are examples of two different situations in which I used the information gathered about my context and my understanding of its meaning to assist me in making decisions about "being my B.E.S.T."

Situation 1: Selecting an office location using information about a significant attribute in my physical surroundings.

Just recently my company moved to a new location. When relocating my office, I had a choice of two suites. Both were the same size, different layouts, and had one side comprised of large windows. Given my understanding that the sun plays a significant role in influencing me to "be my B.E.S.T.," I decided to take its location into consideration prior to making my selection. As I looked at the suites, I determined which of the two was in the location that would receive sunlight in the morning. Suite B became my choice. Now, in the morning upon arrival to work, the sun greets me, my spirit is awakened, and I feel energized and ready to work; I am *Bright*. My days are productive. I *Excel*. At the end of the day, I leave *Satisfied*. Because I am satisfied, so, too, is my partner. Based upon my understanding of my context, an informed choice was made that is helping me to "be my B.E.S.T."

Situation 2: Using information about the people in my life space to assist me in making a business decision.

In one of my periods when the flow of business was slow, I found myself feeling despondent and questioning my sense of direction. To make sure that I did not let these feelings suppress my taking the needed course of action, I decided to contact the one person who I knew had a significant impact on me. I called my mother. At the end of our conversation, I felt more aware of the factors influencing my current business state; I was *Bright*. I had identified the action steps I needed to get my business back on course. I was ready to *Excel*. I knew my mother was proud of me, and her satisfaction always elevated my *Satisfaction*. I was ready to act now. *Time* was of the essence. As always, my mother helped me to focus on "being my B.E.S.T."

Remember, measurement is a form of discovery. It is a process that involves exploring, examining, and investigating. This process often takes us in different directions and toward many paths. It requires that we ask many questions, consider many variables, and ascertain many connections. For some, measuring is interesting, and for others, it is tedious. My intention is that by the end of this book, you will be on the side of "interesting." You will be among those who are eager to learn more about yourself so that you can "be your B.E.S.T." You will join me in recognizing that you can only arrive at your B.E.S.T. destination by embracing a B.E.S.T. practice measurement.

At Your B.E.S.T. Activity

Our physical environment impacts us. Think about where you live, work, learn, volunteer, and have fun. Select one of these environments. Complete the table that reflects your assumptions about what physical attributes and people impact you "being your B.E.S.T."

Discovering My Context

B.E.S.T. Characteristics	Physical Surroundings Attribute	Clue	People	Clue
Bright				
Excellence				
Satisfaction				
Timely				

1. Are there any physical attributes that impact more than one B.E.S.T. characteristic? If yes, which one(s)?
2. Are there any people that impact more than one B.E.S.T. characteristic? If yes, who?
3. What questions will you ask to verify your assumptions about both the physical attributes and people in your environment?
4. What observations will you make to verify your assumptions about both the physical attributes and people in your environment?

5. How will you use the information gained to make more informed decisions?

I recommend that you complete a contextual analysis of all locations in your physical environment. You might discover that some physical attributes and people have significant influence because they impact multiple locations.

Points to Remember

- **Understanding your context and its impact on you is central to you "being your B.E.S.T."** Your environment forms your context. It is comprised of your physical surroundings and the people in your life space. This context influences and shapes you.

- **Attitudes are shaped early in life.** It is essential that you examine your childhood context. People you interacted with in your childhood played a significant role in the values, interests, and attitudes you have today. Therein lays many influencers and shapers of your B.E.S.T.

- **It is easy to make assumptions or guesses about your context.** But to know your context and its impact requires that you measure. Gathering information about your context may affirm your conjecture. It may also provide you with new insights.

- **While measurement is a complex process** that requires asking questions, making observations, and considering variables, it is an integral part of helping you to define and be your B.E.S.T. At the heart of this process is an "inquiring mind."

- **Gathering information is only the first step to being your B.E.S.T.** The next essential step involves utilizing the information gathered to derive meaning and guide you in making the correct choices that will assist you in "being your B.E.S.T."

What will you do with this information to "be your B.E.S.T."?

Chapter 4

Engage in Your B.E.S.T. Acts

Do you "talk the talk" or "walk the talk?"

Being your B.E.S.T. demands that your words and actions are congruent, they match. The first step in aligning the two is to make sure that you are using the words that will call forth your B.E.S.T. What you send out into the universe comes back to you. Hence, you must be mindful of the words you use and your tone of voice. Take a moment and examine your vocabulary. Do you find among the words that you use "can't" and "but?" If so, these two words must be deleted immediately from your vocabulary. They will prevent you from "being your B.E.S.T."

President Barack Obama during his election campaign demonstrated to the world that "words do matter." He was able to galvanize people to support him by first getting them to embrace three simple words—"Yes, we can!" When you use "can" instead of "can't," it signals you believe, have hope, are confident, and conveys a positive spirit. Try it. Repeat the following with passion, enthusiasm, and an emphasis on the words in lettering that is in italics. After each repetition, reflect upon how you feel.

- Yes, *I* can see it! Yes, I *can* see it! Yes, I can *see* it! *Yes*, I can see it!
- Yes, *I* can do it! Yes, I *can* do it! Yes, I can *do* it! *Yes*, I can do it!
- Yes, *I* can make it! Yes, I *can* make it! Yes, I can *make* it! *Yes*, I can make it!
- Yes, *I* can have it! Yes, I *can* have it! Yes, I can *have* it! *Yes*, I can have it!

Repeating "Yes, I can" creates positive energy and is a magnetic force. "Being your B.E.S.T." starts with a vision. Once you have the vision, can see it, and hold on to it knowing that the dream can be realized, you begin to act in ways that will bring your vision to fruition. That is what happened in President Obama's campaign. As people began to believe that he could become president, they began to donate now. They began to work to get people registered to vote. They drove people to the polls. They made a dream a reality. They did it. They elected the first African American president of the United States. They affirmed that "words do matter."

Why not take this lesson and use it to "be your B.E.S.T."? It takes less than sixty seconds to send these three simple words into the universe. The return on this daily habit is tremendous. You will attract the resources, stamina, courage, and fortitude that you need to "be your B.E.S.T." Make "Yes, I can" one of your B.E.S.T. acts. Over the next twenty-one days, every morning when you awake, say "Yes, I can see it!" Then visualize yourself "being your B.E.S.T." Just before you start your work assignment for the day, say "Yes, I can do it!" Then engage in your B.E.S.T. acts and make sure they are in alignment with your words. Toward early afternoon, recharge yourself by saying "Yes, I can make it!" Prior to closing your eyes at the end of the day, say "Yes, I can have it!"

Equally as important as it is for you to use "can," you must release "but." When you get "but" out of your way, you release excuses, limitations, and barriers and free yourself to search for possibilities, solutions, options, and break new ground. You are no longer in prison or bound up, prevented from reaching your destination. You s-t-r-e-t-c-h! When you get "but" out of your way, you are on mission and focused on "being your B.E.S.T."

Getting "but" out of the way requires that you self-monitor what you say. When you hear the word "but," immediately think of "delete" and release it. Replace it with a visual image of a bird that is freely soaring to new heights. Remind yourself that you or no one will put "but" in your way and bind or limit you from "being your B.E.S.T." How many times have you missed an opportunity because you let "but" get in your way? How many times have you stayed in the same place, on the same job, with the same person because you let "but" get in your way? The time is now to get "but" out of your way; make it another B.E.S.T. act.

Like you, the people around you are also sending messages into the universe. Their messages can have an impact upon you as well. Remember, the people around you play a part in shaping and influencing you. Consequently, you must be cognizant of the words they use too. Think about your family members, friends, and coworkers. These are the people that you spend a significant amount of time with over the course of a day, week, months, and years—your lifetime. Do they use words that inspire, encourage, and affirm you? Or do they use words that bring about fear, discourage, deflation, and negation? Why it is that two people can hear the same words and get different outcomes? While you cannot control what others say, you can control how you respond to what you hear.

Here's my example:

> I had a friend to tell me that I would *never* find the man of my dreams. My criteria were *unrealistic*; just *too high*. I chose to let those words be a challenge to me rather than a deterrent. I decided to continue on in pursuit of my dream man. I surely wouldn't find him if I gave up or changed my criteria. Today, I am blessed to be with the man of my dreams.

What others say to you matters. How you choose to respond is what impacts you being your B.E.S.T. Too often we make the mistake of thinking that someone else's words hurt us or made us feel good about ourselves. The reality is that our feelings emerged as a result of how we chose to respond to what others said or did. Remember, you always have a choice. Make sure your antenna is up! So that you can readily recognize how you are choosing to respond to what you hear. This is another B.E.S.T. act.

Something to Think About . . .

- Identify words that you use which impact your B.E.S.T. characteristics.

    - Which words are you using that are hindering you from "being your B.E.S.T."?
    - Which words are you using that are assisting you to "be your B.E.S.T."?

- How can you make repeating "Yes, I can!" as a part of your daily routine?

- What will you do to keep "but" out of your way?

- Think about the people you identified in the previous chapter that shaped and influenced you in childhood.

    - What words did they use that helped you be your B.E.S.T?
    - What words did they use that prevented you from "being your B.E.S.T"?
    - Now think about how you chose to respond to these words. If you responded differently, would you have gotten the same results?

The next B.E.S.T. act that you must adopt is preparation. This act is critical to aligning your words and deeds. Without preparation, achieving your goal consistently is unlikely. In fact, you might identify a myriad of other reasons for not reaching the goal. You just might not recognize that failure to reach the goal was actually tied to this B.E.S.T. act, preparation. Suppose you said you were going to save five dollars a week. At the end of the week, you saved two dollars. The following are examples of reasons that you might name for not reaching the goal:

"I didn't make enough money to save five dollars."

"Other things came up that required me to spend the money I made."

"There was a sale on something I needed. I had to make the purchase because the sale price was only for this week."

You probably can come up with many other reasons. But at the heart of not achieving the goal is most often the lack of adequate preparation. Here is why preparation is important. In this example, preparation would entail deciding how you will save five dollars weekly. What can you realistically do that will result in five dollars saved? Will you give up buying a favorite drink that you currently purchase every morning? Do you take lunch on the days you typically eat out? Preparation entails deciding where to save. Will you put your money in a place that will limit the likelihood that you will use it? Do you put your money to be saved in a piggy bank, house safe, or open a savings account? Preparation also involves determining your method of tracking and accounting of the money saved. How will you know the amount you have saved daily so that your weekly goal is reached? Adequate preparation minimizes unexpected distractions and ensures personal readiness. Preparation gives you an advantage. To create this advantage, it requires that you take time and are thoughtful. That means you may need to take a personal time out. *Stop* being busy and taking action without adequate groundwork. If you want to be your B.E.S.T., then investing time in preparation is significant. This B.E.S.T. act is the catalyst that ignites your actions so that you have the optimal likelihood of making your words a reality.

Something to Think About . . .

- Can you be your B.E.S.T. without preparation?
- What successful people do you know? How much time do they invest in preparation?
- Think about a time when you were at your B.E.S.T. How did preparation align your words and actions?
- Think about a time when you were not at your B.E.S.T. How did you prepare? Was your preparation adequate?

Sometimes, you are unaware of the fact that your actions are not in sync with your words. To minimize these occurrences and/or to ensure that you don't stay out of sync, it is helpful to have a person in your life space that you can count on to be your objective observer. This person needs to be someone who is unafraid to tell you what you may not want to hear. Additionally, this person needs to be someone you will listen to when he or she speaks. For me, it is my husband. He is good at observing whether my behavior is in alignment with my words. We have an agreement that when he sees me acting in ways that are not consistent with my words, he is to call me on it. That means, pointing out the behaviors that are out of sync.

Here's an Example:

My Words: I am going to lose ten pounds.

My Action: Eating my favorite chocolate dessert at 9:00 p.m.

My B.E.S.T. Buddy: Pat, I thought you were working on losing ten pounds?

My Words: I am.

My B.E.S.T. Buddy: Have you noticed you are still eating your favorite dessert at night past 7:00 p.m.?

While I sometimes dislike having to discover that some of my actions are not consistent with my words, having a buddy identify when I am out of sync has forced me to reassess my commitment to my words. This has proven to be invaluable. There have been times that my actions have changed and other times when my words have changed. Having an observation buddy helps you to "be your B.E.S.T." and/or redefine what B.E.S.T. means.

Something to Think About . . .

- Among the people who are currently in your life space, who spends time with you enough to make observations about your actions?
- Given the person or people identified in the previous question, who are you most likely to listen to if they pointed out an action that was inconsistent with your words?
- What would you do if this person informed you of an action that was not in sync with your words?
- What ground rules do you need to establish with your B.E.S.T. buddy to ensure that you listen, receive the feedback in a positive manner, and take action?

During my doctoral studies while working with a long-term stroke patient, I discovered an intervention that triggered my patient's ability to recall and articulate familiar words. Excited about my discovery, the good news was shared immediately with my faculty advisor. Needless to say, my advisor was excited too because this patient had been enrolled in speech therapy for over three years and to date had not uttered a word. What happened next proved to be another important lesson for me. Rather than continuing to implement my intervention, my faculty advisor developed a plan that included providing my intervention for two weeks and then returning to a traditional intervention for two weeks. Over a period of time, both interventions were alternated over two-week intervals. While the patient showed progress over the entire time period, it was during the intervals with my intervention that the greatest progress occurred. As a result of this data gathering, I came to realize that while several actions can facilitate a desired result, not all actions are equal. In other words, some actions bring about results faster; hence are more efficient. Some actions obtain better results; hence more effective. Some actions require that you expend more resources than others; hence more costly.

Here's my example:

I wanted to lose forty pounds within a six-month period. To do so, I connected with an individual who was knowledgeable about weight loss. She informed me this was doable, but I needed to adhere to her regimen. This regimen was comprised of preferred practices and designed to achieve the results in the most efficient manner. First, it was about nutrition-eliminating and adopting new actions. Next, it was about physical activity—increasing amount and type of movement. Starting with nutrition was important because it brought about the most significant weight loss in the shortest amount of time. Hence, I was satisfied, more encouraged and ready to move on to the next key area—physical activity. Matching the type of activity to my interests and lifestyle proved to enhance my weight loss efforts. Again, I was satisfied with the activity and soon had integrated it into my routine and wouldn't let anything get in the way of my physical activity. Within the established timeline, my goal was achieved and I had preferred practices that I could take with me to help me continue to "be my B.E.S.T."

Probably one of the greatest benefits of comparing actions is the realization that identifying "preferred practices" will make certain that you are spending the least amount of time and resources to achieve your greatest result.

Something to Think About . . .

- How often have you examined your actions to determine their influence on your desired outcomes?
- Have you ever compared actions to see if one worked better than the other?

- Think about one result you want to achieve. What acts do you need to engage in that will assist you in achieving your result? Which of these should you compare to determine your "preferred practices?"

Return now to my story and use it to examine the key messages of this chapter.

~

My Story

My teacher knew that arithmetic would be easy for me if I would stop crying and get focused. She had tried everything she knew to get me to change my attitude about arithmetic to no avail. It didn't seem to matter whether she introduced the subject after my favorite activity, reading; paired me with a student who did well in arithmetic; reminded me that I was smart and could do anything. I continued to cry. In fact, my crying had now become disruptive to the class. Other students were overheard laughing and making fun of me. My teacher decided that it was now time to call my mother. She knew my mother from her involvement in the school's parent association.

When my teacher met with my mother, she explained the situation. My mother was surprised because every day she asked me "how I was doing in school?" and I had always said "fine." I had never mentioned crying. My teacher gave my mother a copy of the book that we were using in the classroom. She suggested that my mother use it at home to help me feel more comfortable with the material that she was presenting during class time.

That evening, my mother talked with my dad about her meeting with my teacher. Together they came up with their plan. It involved getting my big brother to help me. Since he periodically checked my homework and I loved sharing my work with him, helping me with my arithmetic could be easily integrated into an existing activity. When they approached him about the situation at hand, he was eager to help. While he enjoyed his time with me, the new responsibility was going to give him an opportunity to practice his teaching skills. My big brother was enrolled in the local college preparing to be an elementary school teacher.

The next day when I arrived home, my mother did not ask her usual questions. This time, she asked me two new ones: What did you do today that went well? What did you do today that didn't go well? I hesitated for a moment but decided to share that I had cried. My mother then asked what made me cry. I told her that I didn't like arithmetic. She queried further what didn't I like about arithmetic. I said that it was hard and that I didn't think I would do as well as I did in my favorite subject, reading.

My mother always had a way of making me feel special and think that I could do anything. So she once again made me feel better. She gave me a big smile as she put her arm around me and said, "I bet you can do arithmetic as well as you can read. You just might have to work a little harder." Then she pulled out the book from class. Just the sight of it brought tears to my eyes. "But why do I have to use that book?" I asked. My mom explained that my big brother was going to come over at least three days and review the book with me. She reminded me how much I liked working with him, and she was certain that he and I together could tackle the book. That was another thing about my mother; she usually had thought about everything. There was generally no out. So I agreed to give it a try. After all, my mother was just asking me to "be my B.E.S.T."

~

At My B.E.S.T. Activity

1. What did my mother say that encouraged me to work on my arithmetic?
2. When did I let "but" get in the way?
3. What best acts does my big brother support?
4. What might my teacher have done differently?
5. What did my mother change to make sure her words were in sync with her actions?
6. How might you measure to determine if having my big brother work with me is a preferred practice?

Go to <u>www.OMGGetsResults.Com</u> to compare your responses with mine.

Points to Remember

Embrace the following six B.E.S.T. acts to assist you in being your B.E.S.T.

- **Affirm "Yes, I can" daily.** Making this affirmation a part of your daily routine will serve as a positive catalyst to attract the resources, stamina, courage, and fortitude that you need to "be your B.E.S.T."

- **Get "but" out of your way.** Eliminating "but" from your vocabulary frees you to find the unlimited possibilities that will lead you to "be your B.E.S.T."

- **Make sure your antenna is up!** Watching how you choose to respond to the words used by others will assist you in letting go of the negative and embracing the positive so that you can "be your B.E.S.T."

- **Prepare for everything.** Take the time to get ready, organize, practice, and train. Adequate preparation is integral to "being your B.E.S.T."

- **Find a B.E.S.T. buddy.** You cannot always recognize when your behaviors are out of sync with your words. Having a person you respect and trust to keep track of your actions and call you on it is necessary if you are to "be your B.E.S.T."

- **Identify your preferred practices.** Not all actions are equal. Determining your preferred practices will help you identify how to spend the least amount of time and resources to "be your B.E.S.T."

What will you do with this information to "be your B.E.S.T."?

Chapter 5

Make Your B.E.S.T. Interpretation

"Being your B.E.S.T." involves making choices on life's journey that will direct you toward your B.E.S.T.

You can only know your B.E.S.T. when you measure. The process of measuring provides you with the critical information needed to assist you in making the right choices. The next critical step after measuring is to determine the meaning and impact of the information collected. The quality of the interpretation of the information collected influences your options. Over the past thirty years, I have observed that relinquishing measurement to others often results in releasing interpretation of results as well. Hence, choices about what to do next are determined and/or influenced by the entity that is measuring. This means that when you rely upon someone other than yourself to interpret the information collected about you, the alternatives proposed are generally tied to their knowledge, experience, and bias. This may result in you making choices that are not right for you and subsequently prevent you from "being your B.E.S.T."

Here's my example:

I was headed home from college for the winter holiday. I asked my mother what was the weather like. She told me it was cold and that I should bring my winter clothes. When I arrived home, it was sixty degrees and all of the clothes that I had were 100 percent wool. I had prepared for "cold" weather. In fact, over the two-week period that I was going to be home, the weatherman was predicting that it would reach seventy-five degrees. Needless to say, I was inadequately prepared. In order for me to be comfortable and engage in the activities that were planned, I had to go shopping for new clothes. What happened? To my mother, sixty degrees was cold. After all, it was Florida, and a forty-degree drop in the temperature made it feel "cold." Unlike my mother who had always lived in the south, I was attending college in Michigan. Now that I was in the Midwest, sixty degrees was "warm" after the bitter, blustering twenty-and-below weather I had been experiencing. The clothes that I had taken with me were not suitable for the Michigan winters. During the course of winter, I had bought clothes there so that I could be warm. This visit helped me to realize that I now really owned "winter clothes." Had I collected the information about the weather during my break versus relying on my mother's interpretation of the temperature, I would have made a different choice about clothing. My experience and knowledge about weather conditions was no longer the same as my mother's, and that difference would have led me to different choices which would have saved a few dollars too.

Something to Think About . . .

- What might I have done to verify that my mother had interpreted the information correctly from my perspective?
- How might I have determined if my mother's personal experience and/or bias were influencing her interpretation of the weather?
- How might my choices have impacted me "being my B.E.S.T.?"

When you are analyzing data, you are organizing it in a manner that is understandable and useful for extracting meaning, interpretation. Interpretation involves constructing a logical argument that explains the data. Your interpretation represents your inferences, suggestions, or hypotheses about the data. Generally, the basis for your interpretation is your personal expertise and experience. It is your interpretation that influences your choices. Let's take a look at another personal example to further explore analysis and interpretation.

Here's my example:

My Impending Trip

Before I pack for a business trip, I collect a variety of data (information): the weather forecast; my itinerary; dress requirements—which clothes are in my closet, comfortable, and fit; which clothes take up less room in my suitcase and are wrinkle free when I pack, etc. On a trip headed to Chicago to work with a client, the weather forecast was forty-eight degrees with intermittent rain showers over the two days that I was scheduled to be there. The first day included meeting in my client's office with the two project leaders. It was Friday and their dressed down, casual day. While the client had not scheduled anything for the evening, I was going to spend that time meeting with the consultant whom I was working with the next day. We needed to review the work plan and materials, ensure that roles were clearly defined, and affirm our strategy. The retreat we were facilitating was going to be held at a conference facility at one of the local parks. It was starting early Saturday morning and expected to conclude by six in the evening. The board members participating had agreed to casual dress. On Sunday, the next day, I had to leave early in order to get back for a church program that my pastor had scheduled me to be a participant. My plane was scheduled to land at 10:25 a.m. It was time to spring forward, daylight savings time was changing on Sunday.

My Analysis

During the time I was scheduled to be in Chicago, it was going to be cool. I would be spending most of my time inside working and would likely not experience much of the wet weather if it did rain. Even though it appeared that casual clothes would be appropriate, as the consultant it was my preferred practice to dress professionally at all times. I wanted to maintain a certain decorum and recognition as a professional. I was going to lose an hour's sleep the morning I was departing because the time was moving forward an hour. If the plane landed as scheduled, I would have thirty-five minutes to get off the plane to my car and drive to my church.

While organizing the data, you are likely to discover if there are missing data. For example, in this situation it would have been useful to know the typical arrival time of this flight. From that data, I would be able to determine if the plane had a history of on-time arrivals or not. In other words, was there a pattern of being on time or late? Sometimes, your data analysis is subjective based upon your personal knowledge and experience. In this example, it is my personal experience with clients that is influencing my analysis regarding the impact of professional consultants' clothes on their clients. Is my perception shared by other professional consultants? Verification of data is important especially when your analysis is subjective.

My Interpretation

Since it is going to be cool, I will not need winter clothing.

I will need to take something that will protect me from the rain just in case I am outside when it rains.

Dressy casual clothes will be appropriate except when I meet with my colleague and Sunday when I will need something dressy for church.

I must make sure that my clocks are changed to reflect the new time so that the alarm is set for the correct time.

There is no room for error either leaving Chicago or upon arrival at my home airport.

Since I am on the church program, I must be dressed for church; the plane must leave and arrive on time so that I can head straight to church in time for the start of service.

In general, when you interpret data, you look for impact and implications. For example, my interpretation of the weather condition influenced my determination regarding the type of clothing to pack for my trip. Relationships are considered so that you can explain trends and uncover patterns. In this situation, comparing the plane's arrival time over time would allow be to uncover a pattern; if the pattern was 80 percent on time, then you might hypothesize that it is likely that my plane would arrive in time for me to get to my church program. Given the weather conditions in my city are similar to Chicago's and I have been living in the Midwest for fifteen years, I interpreted the weather as "cool." My interpretation was based upon my personal experience. Remember my previous experience with sixty-degree weather in the previous chapter.

My Choices

I decided to take:

- An all-weather coat with lining and a hood. I made this selection so that I would be warm, protected from the rain, and could easily navigate during the rainy, intermittent periods.
- Two traveler's pant suits which were professional and yet could be considered casual. Additionally, they were comfortable, wrinkle free, and wouldn't take up much room in my suitcase.
- A pair of jeans and sweater to wear when meeting with my colleague for the evening. I would be comfortable, warm, and relaxed.
- A black two-piece that was wrinkle free and was appropriate for church.
- One piece of luggage that would fit over head and could be carried on the plane.

I also decided to:

- Set my phone alarm, room clock alarm, and scheduled a hotel wake-up call to ensure I woke up at the right time.
- Schedule airport pickup the night before to ensure I had transportation to the airport at the time I needed it.

Given my analysis and interpretation of the information gathered, coupled with my experience in traveling, I was able to make choices that helped me to "be my B.E.S.T."

Be mindful that expertise and experience are two key factors that contribute to the quality of your choices. Hence, when you have limited expertise and experience in a specific area, it is important that you complete additional data gathering or research. You can do this by talking with someone who is an expert or has experience in the area and/or by gathering and reviewing information that has been published in a reputable source.

Let's return to my story so that you can put your new knowledge to work and interpret my current status.

~

My Story

It has been six weeks since my parents implemented their plan.

Three times a week my big brother came over after school to help me with my arithmetic. He had a way of making me feel special. I don't know whether it was his voice that was always calming, or his big smile that warmed my heart, or his attentiveness when I was sharing my news of the day.

My big brother arrived for our first session with a big poster board. I couldn't imagine what we were going to do with it. He explained that we were going to create a scorecard so that we could track my progress. Together, we talked about what would go on the scorecard. First, we agreed on what time period we were going to measure. I thought we could measure over the next six weeks which would take us to the end of my grading period. He thought that was a good idea. Then we talked about what activities that we should track and why that was easy. It seemed like my homework would be one. He suggested my test scores from class. And since we were working together until the end of the grading period, I thought we could also use my class grade. He added tracking the activities we did together beyond the homework. Now we were all set. I cut out pictures and pasted them on the poster board. Together, we made the scorecard and hung it over my desk so that I could easily see it.

To get me to like my arithmetic book, my big brother let me in on a big secret. It was good that I had the book that was used in school. If I reviewed the book with him, I would be prepared for class. And if I really went further than the teacher asked me, I might even get ahead of my classmates. Now he knew just what to say. I was very competitive and always wanted to be first in my class.

Right from the start, he began working with me using my strength, reading. He reintroduced my arithmetic book to me as a storybook filled with both words and numbers. My task was to read the words, and his task was to help me understand the numbers. I quickly got connected with the book because I loved to read. Within a week, I was no longer crying at the sight of the book.

His task was to give me an assignment with the numbers, and my task was to find words that related to them in my arithmetic book. By the second week, I saw my book as valuable and was eager to look inside. In fact, when I found an answer, I got to put a star on our scorecard.

By the third week, I had gotten stars daily. Up to this point, my big brother had been helping me with my homework. Now my task was to complete the homework without any help. His task was to review and grade the homework. Each time I completed my homework without any help, I got a star. By the fourth week, I had stars indicating that all homework had been completed without any help.

My big brother thought that since I was doing so well, he would reduce the number of days he came over to work with me. We agreed that he would come over one day during the school week and one day on the weekend. On the weekend, he and I would review the work completed during the week and then preview the week ahead. We did two days a week for the next three weeks. At the end of the third week, there were stars on my scoreboard. All of my homework had been completed. My big brother had to study for his tests. So I was on my own for the next week. And to my surprise, I completed all my homework and made an "A" on the pop quiz in class. When my big brother stopped over the next week, I shared the good news. He was excited to know that I did so well on my own. In fact, he thought it was time now for me to continue to do my work without him. After all, my actions clearly demonstrated that I was ready to go it alone. If by chance some problems did arise, my big brother reminded me that he was just a phone call away.

Seeing all the stars on my scoreboard brought personal satisfaction. The stars reminded me that most of my homework had been completed without any assistance. Since my first birthday, according to my mother, being independent was important to me. My confidence was up, and it showed in the classroom. All of my pop quiz scores had been As. This reporting period, I was certain that my arithmetic grade would be an "A."

My teacher had a new problem. Rather than crying, now I didn't want arithmetic to end.

～

At My B.E.S.T. Activity

1. How would you organize the information about my current status so that you can get meaning about my progress? Is there any missing data?
2. What trends or patterns emerged? How did these impact my classroom performance?
3. How confident can you be in your interpretation of my current status?
4. What interpretation supported my big brother's choices?
5. Based upon your interpretation, was I "being my B.E.S.T."?

Go to www.OmgGetsResults.com and share your responses.

Points to Remember

- **Analysis involves organizing the information you have collected in a manner that will allow you to derive meaning.** Before you can interpret your results, you must put the information or data into an order that tells a story. Don't forget that numbers tell a story just like words.

- **Confidence in your interpretation is contingent upon having complete and accurate information.** Sometimes in the process of analyzing, you will find that you have incomplete and inaccurate information. When this is the case, you must make note of the influence of these factors in your interpretation because the quality of your interpretation will have been compromised. Before you move to interpretation, it will be worth your while to collect the additional information or data that you need.

- **Your expertise, experience, and bias influence your interpretation of information.** Be mindful when you rely upon others' interpretation because it is similarly being influenced by their expertise, experience, and bias. You must be mindful of these factors so that you make the interpretation that will lead you to "be your B.E.S.T."

- **The quality of your interpretation impacts the quality of your choices.** The more accurate your interpretation of information, the more likely you are to make choices that will lead you to your B.E.S.T.

- **Making your B.E.S.T. interpretation is essential to ensuring you make the right choices that will result in you "being your B.E.S.T."** Interpretation is a critical next step after measuring because it involves determining meaning and impact. It forms the basis for making correct choices that will assist you in "being your B.E.S.T."

What will you do with this information to "be your B.E.S.T."?

Chapter 6

Share Your B.E.S.T. Results

Are you a B.E.S.T. kept secret? Through my many years of working with individuals and organizations, one constant that I have found is that most have not taken the time to tell their story. Some of the most common reasons shared with me may be familiar to you as well.

- I don't have the time.
- I have been busy doing the work.
- I don't know how to tell my story.
- I don't want to appear as though I am bragging.
- I don't want to be perceived as arrogant.
- I thought my work would speak for itself.
- I don't have the resources to tell my story.
- I don't know who should hear my story.

The benefits of telling your story are bountiful. Not only do you benefit, but so do those with whom you share, and potentially many others, some of whom you will never know.

Here's my example:

I was invited to keynote a faculty institute, at a university, for the purpose of getting the faculty to embrace the value of outcomes measurement. Thinking about how to best present the information in a way that a diverse group of faculty would understand and connect resulted in a decision to use a personal analogy as part of my introductory remarks. After being introduced by the provost, my lecture began with me sharing my B.E.S.T.

My Personal Analogy

Periodically, I would say to my husband, "I really need to lose some weight."

After observing me for a while, my husband said to me, "You don't practice what you preach."

I asked him, "What did you mean?"

He said, "You go around working with people and telling them that they must measure to get results and you won't even get on the scale."

I said, "I do measure—I know when my clothes get too tight that it's time for me to do something."

Well, he knew how to get my attention. He knew how passionate I am about measurement and results and knew that if he brought it to my attention I would do something.

When I thought about it from my outcomes measurement perspective, here is what I realized:

(1) I didn't know what my outcome should be. Was it losing some weight? If so, how much did I need to lose? Was it to maintain a healthy lifestyle? Or did I want to be physically healthy?
(2) I wasn't using the right measure? Clearly using my clothes as a barometer was not allowing me to be efficient? By the time they were snug, I would have to work harder to reach my goal.
(3) I didn't know if weight was the best indicator of success since I wasn't really certain about my outcome.

After spending some time reflecting and conducting my personal needs assessment, I realized that my ultimate outcome was to be healthy, but to get there required me to identify other outcomes. I began putting into practice what I do daily with organizations, and I can truly say—"that which gets measured gets managed." Based upon my personal data, I modified my lifestyle and incorporated measurement into my daily activities.

When I get up in the morning, I weigh—results influence my behavior for the day.

I use a pedometer at least three times per week to track my total number of daily steps. (I was wearing my pedometer and opened my jacket so that they could see it.) Results help me to step more each day. When I think about the food I am going to eat, I count the calories. I have purchased a new machine that allows me to measure my body fat and body mass index and do that monthly.

I report my results in a variety of ways to my personal coach, husband, friends, and, yes, even to my clients.

I have lost thirty-five pounds within a four-month period. Note, I know the exact weight loss over a specific time period.

This example supports my basic mantra that I want to share with you today—"that which gets measured gets managed."

After my analogy, to my surprise, the faculty gave me a standing ovation. You could sense the energy and readiness to listen to my outcomes lecture. Several faculty members came up to me afterward and indicated that the personal analogy really helped to get them focused on the importance of measurement. About six months later, I was on the campus and an individual came up to me and said, "I still remember 'that which gets measured gets managed.' Your lecture helped me in a personal way as well. I was inspired to do something about my health. I have now reached my goal weight."

In this example, the faculty gained new information that if used would lead to faculty members examining methods used to evaluate their performance and measuring to ensure their teaching, and student outcomes were achieved. Subsequently, sharing with the faculty could ultimately benefit their students whom I would never know. What I learned from sharing occurred from my accidental connection with the faculty member upon a return-campus visit. Sharing my story had a personal benefit as well. Someone's life had been touched.

Sharing with others propels both you and those that you share to do something. New knowledge is gained from sharing, and that knowledge can lead to self-improvement. Sharing with others can result in others being encouraged, inspired, and hopeful. Sharing with others can assist others in becoming their B.E.S.T.

Something to Think About . . .

- Identify a situation that you have shared a personal story.

  - Who did you share it with?
  - What were your personal benefits from sharing?
  - How did those you shared your story with benefit?
  - What new knowledge did you gain from sharing?
  - How did you use that new knowledge?

- Identify a situation that someone shared their personal story.

  - How did you benefit from their sharing?
  - How did their sharing make you feel? Were you encouraged, inspired, and hopeful?

- What new knowledge did you gain from sharing?
- How did you use that new knowledge?

Have you ever heard "there is no need in reinventing the wheel"? If we know that something works, then why not use it? In fact today, many funders are requiring organizations to use evidence-based practices. This is a requirement because the funder wants to ensure a return on investment as quickly as possible. Hence, if an organization uses a practice that is known to bring about results versus one that is not, the funder is certain that goals will be achieved faster and costs will be contained. This same concept can be applied to personal sharing. Sharing your B.E.S.T. with others can assist in saving time, resources, and achieving goals faster.

Here's my example:

I had a prospective client that was hosting a conference within a week and needed an evaluation tool to ensure their outcomes were achieved. They wanted someone who could provide the tool quickly and at a nominal cost. This was definitely something I could do. And it was all because of sharing.

For over twenty-five years, my husband had been involved in meeting planning. During that time period, he had planned meetings for his professional association both within and outside the United States. Additionally, he had been an active member of a meeting planner association, attending their professional development conferences twice a year. Because of my evaluation work, he always shared with me information about meeting evaluation, including issues, tools, and resources. As a result, I had developed a meeting evaluation tool kit. It was easy for me to access the information and tools needed to meet this prospective client's needs. Because the groundwork had been done, my costs could be competitive. I submitted my proposal and won the bid.

Something to Think About . . .

- Identify a situation that you shared a story that helped someone save time, resources, and/or achieve their goals.
  - How did the person you share with benefit?

- Identify a situation that someone shared a story with you that helped you save time, resources, and/or achieve their goals.
  - How did you benefit?

Sharing your B.E.S.T. helps you "be your B.E.S.T." You learn from those you share with, and they learn from you. Sharing your B.E.S.T. also helps those you share with become their B.E.S.T., and when they share, others discover their B.E.S.T. Just by sharing your B.E.S.T. you can have an exponential impact on others being their B.E.S.T.

Let's return now to my story and see how easily you identify the benefits of sharing.

~

My Story

I could hardly wait to get home and tell my mother that I had made an "A" on my final arithmetic test. She gave me a big hug and told me how proud she was of me. Then the phone rang. It was my big brother. He knew it was my test day. My mother told him, "Patricia has good news to share," and handed me the phone. Enthusiastically, I shouted, "I did it! I made an 'A' on my arithmetic test." "Good for you," my big brother replied. "You have worked real hard to earn that 'A.'" He then asked, "What did your teacher say about that grade?" I eagerly replied, "She was pleased with the progress I had made. She also wanted to know what I had been doing to get such a good grade. I explained that you had been helping me at home and that I was keeping score of my work. I also told her that I was doing so good that you didn't need to come over as much anymore." "Sounds like you might not need me at all," replied my big brother. "I'll let you know after I get my next assignment." While I had him on the phone, I asked my mother if he could come over and celebrate my "A" with us. She thought that was a good idea and suggested that we all celebrate when Dad got home. She was certain he would be pleased to hear the good news as well. My big brother agreed to come over later. As my mother and I were preparing for the celebration, she asked me one of her favorite questions: Had I done my best? My mother reminded me that the "A" had indicated my performance on the test had placed me in an excellent range. She wanted me to think about if I had done everything that I could do to "be my best." My first thought was I had because of the "A." But the more I thought about it, I realized that when I finished the test I didn't go over my answers. I just handed in my test because I felt confident that I had done well. While a 94 was great and certainly my highest score yet on an arithmetic test, it did mean that I had missed something on the test. Perhaps the next time I should cross-check my work before handing it in to my teacher. Who knows, maybe I could have gotten a perfect score? That was my mother, always challenging me to think about my best.

~

At My B.E.S.T. Activity

How did I benefit from sharing my story?

How might my big brother have benefited?

How might my teacher have benefited?

How might I improve as a result of my sharing?

Go to www.OMGGetsResults.Com and share your responses.

Points to Remember

- **Make it a point to share.** Don't keep your B.E.S.T. to yourself. Every day make sure you share your B.E.S.T. with someone.

- **Make time to share.** When deciding how to spend your time, make allowances for sharing. Sharing your B.E.S.T. is an important part of how you spend your time.

- **Learn from sharing.** Listen to understand the feedback you receive from those with whom you share. Identify new ideas, information, and actions.

- **Improve from sharing.** Use the feedback you receive to get better. Life is about continually improving.

- **Celebrate sharing.** Think of ways you can acknowledge sharing. It can be as simple as a hug.

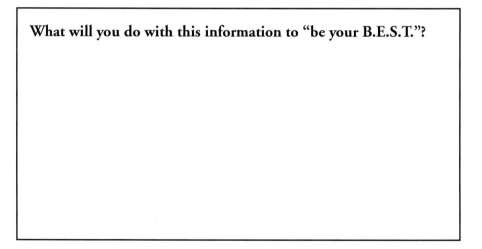

What will you do with this information to "be your B.E.S.T."?

Chapter 7

Develop and Execute Your B.E.S.T. Plan

A personal roadmap is needed so that you will remain focused on "being your B.E.S.T." This roadmap is your B.E.S.T. plan. Without a plan, life happens, opportunities come and go, gifts are locked within and underutilized, and you can't "be your B.E.S.T." Having a written plan is an important first step to ensuring you have defined a course of action that can lead you to your desired outcomes. It becomes the blueprint that facilitates you taking charge of your life. Today, more than ever, time is limited and resources are scarce. Both are key drivers to accomplishing results. Having a written plan will help you to establish priorities, identify the support you will need, make the best use of your time, and manage your resources effectively.

Your B.E.S.T. plan is designed to empower you and propel you to take action.

Desired Outcomes

The starting point of developing your B.E.S.T. plan is *defining your desired outcomes*. In other words, what do you want to achieve over the time period of your plan? You will need to define your time period. Are you planning for a year, two years, three years, or five? If you have determined your *personal mission*, then your outcomes should be tied to it. They should also be tied to the key aspects of your life (for example, family, finishing college, career, finance, health, stewardship, etc.) that you identify as important during this planning period. If you have yet to discover your mission, then tie your outcomes to the key aspects in your life. Your outcomes are measurable results that you want to celebrate and be recognized for having achieved.

Here's my example that is tied to my mission:

My Mission
To assist individuals and organizations in achieving their desired results.

My Desired Outcomes

By 2015:
- at least fifty thousand people will read "Be Your B.E.S.T."
- at least five thousand people will report results achieved as a direct result of "Be Your B.E.S.T."
- at least one hundred organizations will report results achieved as a direct result of "Be Your B.E.S.T."
- mentored twenty-five best practitioners that achieve their desired results

Here's my example that is tied to the key aspects of my life:

Key Aspects of My Life

- ☐ Spiritual
- ☐ Health
- ☐ Marriage
- ☐ Finances
- ☐ Relationships

My Desired Outcomes

By 2015:
- Maintained balance between mind, body, and spirit
- Be healthy, free of disease, and at my ideal body weight
- Both spouse and I are satisfied with our relationship
- Generated diverse revenue mix sufficient to retire
- Maintained satisfying relationships with family members and friends

Key Areas of Focus

Given your desired outcomes, the next step is to identify the key areas that you must direct your attention in order to achieve your desired outcomes. Try to limit the number of your areas so that you can stay focused and be successful. My preference is not to exceed five. This is often difficult because our tendency is to always "want to do too much."

Here's my example for my mission:

My Key Areas

- Marketing
- Measuring
- Mentoring

If my goal is to reach fifty thousand people through my book, then it would seem reasonable that focusing on marketing the book is essential. This means, I must make sure I am engaged in activities that will get my book in front of enough people so that at least fifty thousand will actually purchase it. Given my desired result that my readers do something with the information shared and actually achieve their results, it becomes important that I engage in some form of measuring to keep track of my readers and the results they achieve that are attributed to my book. To ensure that someone other than myself is sharing the B.E.S.T. message, then focusing on mentoring others to become B.E.S.T. practitioners is also important.

Remember, you have limited time and resources. To ensure that you achieve your desired results and "be your B.E.S.T.," you must remain focused. Limiting your key areas will help you to do just that. You also want to maintain balance; you want to make sure that your mind, body, and spirit are aligned. Balance is also a critical factor to "being your B.E.S.T." Keeping your focus on no more than five key areas will also allow you to have the time to make sure you are nurturing your mind, body, and spirit.

Here's my example for the key aspects of my life:

My Key Areas

- Healthy activities
- Communication
- Financial management

Goals

The next element of your plan involves establishing goals for each of your key areas. The following are characteristics of goal statements. You want your goals to be S.M.A.R.T.

*S*pecific: Anyone should be able to read your goal statement and understand what it means.

*M*easurable: Your goal statement should be written in a manner that you know what needs to be measured in order to determine you have achieved the goal.

*A*chievable: Your goal statement should be something that is doable, something you can complete or attain.

*R*ealistic: Your goal statement is reasonable and rational.

*T*ime bound: Your goal statement should include a specific time that you expect to reach your goal.

S.M.A.R.T. goals facilitate you "being your B.E.S.T."

As you set your goals, this is the time you must be brutally honest with yourself. Where are you in relationship to your envisioned future? Don't pull any punches. The more honest you are with yourself, the more progress you will see. This is the time to identify your strengths, your gifts. Write them down. Specifically, identify what you do well. You might want to get feedback from others who know you well. Sometimes others see things that you do not.

Here's my example:

During my professional career, I worked at the American Speech-Language-Hearing Association. In my position, I brought together professionals from around the country who were recognized experts in specific areas of speech-language pathology scope of practice. These individuals served on committees that were given various charges by the association's governing board. My responsibility was to assist them in accomplishing their charge. After several meetings, my supervisor and I began receiving letters from the committee chairs and members. The following are excerpts from several of them:

> "Pat kept a rather disparate crew on topic and goal-oriented, encouraging appropriate discussion but limiting unproductive and divergent agendas."

> "I thought it was a very productive meeting. I appreciate your outcome-process approach and will certainly implement what I have learned from you. Your timing throughout the meeting was exquisite!

You gave us time to process, time to think out loud, and time to focus. Well done!"

"Pat's ability to guide and direct such an energetic and diverse group is most impressive."

Over time, the specific feedback from participants in my committees helped me to identify my facilitation of diverse groups as a gift and strength. Insights from others can be very enlightening.

Setting realistic goals also requires that you examine your weaknesses. What is it that you aren't doing as well as you should? Where are there areas that you can improve and get better?

Here's my example:

The president of the health care company that I worked called me into his office one day to share some feedback he had received from other members of the executive team. The word among my peers was that I was not a "team player." He reminded me that working with the team was essential to our organization's performance and commitment to our shareholders. As such, he felt I needed to work on my teaming skills. I couldn't believe my ears. How could my peers think that about me? I thought that I was a team player.

So I began my data gathering. I sought out the feedback from my peers to understand what behaviors were giving them that impression. After all, "perception is reality." I soon came to understand, while I was working hard to ensure that my department achieved its goals, my peers felt that I was trying to outshine them. They had these and other ideas about me because I had not taken the time to build a relationship with them. They didn't know who I was beyond their professional colleague, and neither did I know them. My mentor during those days taught me "relationships = results." So an area that I needed to work on was building and cultivating relationships. It wasn't all about doing the work. That lesson has proved invaluable to me.

Sometimes it may be difficult to accept what others identify as your weakness. It is important that you use the skills discussed in chapter two and seek clarification. You must also listen actively. In this case, I listened to understand specifically what behaviors or actions were contributing to their perception. Regardless to whether their view is correct or not, it means that you must do something to change the view. If not, the view will impact your ability to achieve your desired results. None of us are perfect. We all have blemishes that need attention. Understanding your weaknesses is critical to ensuring you set goals for yourself that are realistic and achievable.

Remember to write down your gifts, strengths, and weaknesses. Keep these before you as you think about your goals. Ask yourself, "Given my strengths and weaknesses, what is it that I can reasonably expect to achieve?" and "How long will it take me?"

Here's my example pertaining to my mission:

Key Area:　Mentoring

Goals:　To establish a B.E.S.T. mentoring program by 7/31/11
　　　　　　To mentor twenty-five B.E.S.T. practitioners by 9/30/15

Here's my example pertaining to the key aspects of my life:

Key Area:　Healthy activities

Goals:　To develop a mental and physical regimen that will sustain a healthy lifestyle by 12/31/10

　　　　　To maintain a healthy mental and physical status by 12/31/15

In my examples, both long and short-term goals are identified. My recommendation for goal setting is to establish what you want to achieve over the long-term first and then back into what needs to occur first. Let what you want to achieve ultimately (long-term goal) guide your decision making around goals.

Before moving on in the planning process, share them with someone who knows you—a B.E.S.T. buddy. See if your B.E.S.T buddy can understand your goals without any explanation. If your buddy can, then your goal statement has passed the first test. It is specific. Next, see what your B.E.S.T. buddy thinks you will measure to determine if your goal has been achieved. If your buddy can identify what will be measured, then your goal statement has passed the next test. It is measurable. Now ask your B.E.S.T. buddy if the timelines and goal itself appear realistic. If the answer is yes, the goal statement is realistic. Finally, you want to determine if your B.E.S.T. buddy thinks you can achieve the goal. If the answer is yes, the goal statement is achievable. You can now feel fairly confident that S.M.A.R.T. goals have been established.

Something to Think About . . .

- What is your life's purpose? If you don't know yet, how will you go about determining your purpose? What aspects of your life are important to you?
- Identify a time period that you want to make sure you want to focus on being your B.E.S.T. Is it over the next year, two years, three, five? What specifically do you want to achieve at the end of this time period?
- What are your gifts and strengths? How did you measure to determine? How does your context impact your gifts and strengths?
- What are your weaknesses? What do you need to improve about yourself? How did you measure to determine? How does your context impact your weaknesses?

Having clarity about your purpose and what is important to you drives your B.E.S.T. plan and forms the foundation from which you decide what it is you want to accomplish. In other words, your desired outcomes are tied to your life's assignment and/or the aspects of your life that are most important to you. These results form the basis for setting long and short-term goals. Your goals must be specific, measurable, achievable, realistic, and time bound (S.M.A.R.T.) in order to attain your desired outcomes. You have established the framework that will guide you to "be your B.E.S.T."

Actions

It is time now in the planning process to align your actions with your words. In other words, "What are you going to do to achieve your goals?" Refer back to chapter four and use your discoveries to assist you in defining your actions.

Here's my example pertaining to my mission:

Key Area: Mentoring

Goals: To establish a B.E.S.T. mentoring program by 7/31/11

To mentor twenty-five B.E.S.T. practitioners by 9/30/15

Actions

Daily Affirmations

- Daily when I wake up, I will say, "Yes, I can see my B.E.S.T. mentoring program making a difference in the lives of others."
- Daily as I start my day, I will say, "Yes, I can develop my B.E.S.T. mentoring program so that it will benefit others."
- Daily as I work on my mentoring program, I will say, "Yes, I can complete my B.E.S.T. mentoring program by 7/31/2011."

- Daily, as I prepare for bed, I will say, "Yes, I can make others aware of my B.E.S.T. mentoring program."

Preparation

- Identify successful mentoring programs.
- Collect information and examples of these programs.
- Determine characteristics that made these mentoring programs successful.
- Identify which characteristics will make the B.E.S.T. mentoring program successful.
- Determine what resources were used.
- Identify what resources will be needed for the B.E.S.T. mentoring program to be successful.
- Identify evaluation tools used to measure mentoring programs.
- Determine what evaluation tools will be used to measure the B.E.S.T. mentoring program.

During preparation, you will be engaged in measuring. Remember to refer to chapter two.

Development of the B.E.S.T. Mentoring Program

- Based upon my analysis and interpretation of the information obtained from my preparation activities, I will then identify the specific actions that must be undertaken, when I will complete them, and how I will measure that I completed the appropriate actions on time.

Remember to refer to chapter five to assist you in developing your B.E.S.T. interpretation.

Here's my example pertaining to the key aspects of my life:

Key Area: Healthy Activities

Goals: To develop a mental and physical regimen that will sustain a healthy lifestyle by 12/31/10

               To maintain a healthy mental and physical status by 12/31/15

Actions

Daily Affirmations

- Daily when I wake up, I will say, "Yes, I can see myself healthy, both mentally and physically."
- Daily as I start my day, I will say, "Yes, I can develop my mental and physical regimen so that I can maintain a healthy lifestyle."
- Daily as I work on defining my mental and physical regimen, I will say, "Yes, I can complete the development of my mental and physical regimen by 12/31/2010."
- Daily as I prepare for bed, I will say, "Yes, I can have a healthy lifestyle."

Preparation

- Assess current health status and lifestyle.
- Based upon assessment results, identify what healthy activities are appropriate to improve and/or maintain health status.
- Determine which healthy activities can be integrated into lifestyle and/or changes that need to be made in current lifestyle to accommodate healthy activities.
- Identify what resources will be needed.
- Determine what evaluation tools will be used to measure the impact of healthy activities.

During preparation, you will be engaged in measuring. Remember to refer to chapter two.

Development of Mental and Physical Regimen

- Based upon my analysis and interpretation of the information obtained from my preparation activities, I will then identify the specific actions that must be undertaken, when I will complete them, and how I will measure that I completed the appropriate actions on time.

Remember to refer to chapter five to assist you in developing your B.E.S.T. interpretation.

If you are to achieve your goals, your words and behaviors must be consistent. Decide first what your appropriate affirmations will be and when you will say to them. Remember the "law of attraction," you will get what you send into the universe. Next, make sure you do adequate preparation so that you select the actions that are appropriate for you. Adequate preparation helps you save time in that through your discovery you will determine if there has already been an identification of "best" or "preferred" practices. This will prevent trial and error on your part.

Resources

During preparation, you will have identified the resources that you need. For each resource, you must determine if you already have the resource or have access to it. If not, you must decide how and when you can obtain the resource. Make sure that the time it takes to obtain your resources has been taken into consideration with regard to the timelines identified to complete the actions.

Measurement

Preparation is an important action because it is during preparation that you will also determine how best to measure; that is, what needs to be measured, what tools to measure, and when to measure. Refer to chapters two and five.

Having a plan provides you with a deliberate and intentional roadmap toward becoming your B.E.S.T. Yet we live in an environment that constantly changes. These changes impact us. Priorities change. People in our life space change. Resources change. Timelines change. Ultimately, our plans change. View your plan as dynamic, and be flexible.

Equally important to having a plan is executing. Your ability to execute your plan successfully will be, in part, influenced by your context, your environment. Look back at your analysis in chapter three. What attributes did you identify that you needed in your physical environment to "be your B.E.S.T?" What people did you identify that you need to be around in order to "be your B.E.S.T?" Now decide how you will make sure you utilize the attributes and people to execute your plan.

Here's my example:

The sun is an important attribute in my physical environment that influences me being my B.E.S.T. As I prepared to write this book, I chose to develop my outline sitting in my beach chair on my favorite beach. The sun, roaring waves, and seagulls taking flight brought satisfaction and inspiration. My office was the location that I used to write this book. It was the best place for me because I had access to all the tools I needed and at the same time had the benefit of the sunlight piercing through my picture windows.

While writing my book, my husband was my B.E.S.T. buddy to ensure that I stayed on track and met my timelines. He also reviewed the book when it was completed. I also selected people in my life space to review and give me feedback that I knew could be counted on to complete their review when needed and at the same time would be objective and forthright in their feedback.

Executing requires that you are disciplined and focused. You must prepare for each day, and you do what needs to be done. You send words into the universe that calls forth what you need.

You maintain balance between your mind, body, and spirit. You constantly measure, interpret, and share your results. Additionally, establish a planning calendar that identifies the actions that must be completed according to your plan. Make sure you determine milestones so that you will do what is necessary to complete actions on time. Utilize your B.E.S.T. buddy to hold you accountable for executing. You might also establish a time when you both will review your performance. See the B.E.S.T. execution checklist. Use it to ensure that you are doing what needs to be done to guarantee you achieve your desired outcomes.

Plan and execute your plan so that you can "be your B.E.S.T."

Something to Think About . . .

- Since preparation is a B.E.S.T. act, how will you prepare for developing your B.E.S.T. plan?
- Who will be your B.E.S.T. buddy as you develop your plan?
- What physical attributes and people will you consider as you begin to plan?
- How will you use your planning calendar so that you manage your time appropriately?

My B.E.S.T. Execution Checklist

- ☐ Review my mission, key aspects of life, and desired outcomes
- ☐ Develop my action list for the day in concert with my plan
- ☐ Repeat my affirmations
- ☐ Be positive
- ☐ Nourish my spirit
- ☐ Make healthy food choices
- ☐ Get moving for at least twenty minutes
- ☐ Check the attributes of my physical environment
- ☐ Assess the impact of the people around me
- ☐ Do what is on my action list for the day
- ☐ Measure
- ☐ Interpret
- ☐ Share Results
- ☐ Prepare for the next day

My < > B.E.S.T. Plan
(Insert the time period for the plan.)

You can go to <u>www.OmgGetsResults.com</u> to complete your B.E.S.T. plan online.

My Personal Mission *(Write your personal mission statement here.)*

```
┌─────────────────────────────────────────────────────┐
│                                                       │
│                                                       │
│                                                       │
└─────────────────────────────────────────────────────┘
```

The Important Aspects of My Life *(List below the aspects of your life that are most important to you over this planning period.)*

Desired Outcomes *(What results do you want to achieve as they relate to your mission? What about the important aspects of your life? Again, think about these within the time period of this plan.)*

Key Areas *(What major areas do you need to direct your attention if you are to achieve your desired outcomes?) Remember to keep these to four to five.*

Mission

Key Life Aspects

Goals *(What do you need to accomplish in order to attain your desired outcomes? Think first about the end of your planning period.)*

Long-Term Goals

Short-Term Goals

Affirmations *(What will you affirm daily?)*

Preparation (*What will you do to make sure you select the appropriate actions, resources, and measures?*)

Actions

Actions (Tasks to be completed/ categorized by goal)	Resources Needed (what, availability, cost)	Timeline (start-end date)	Measures (what, when, tool)

Context

Attributes of Physical Environment	People (Make sure you identify a B.E.S.T. buddy.)

Chapter 8

Create Your B.E.S.T. Reward

Think about your conversation with family members, friends, coworkers, and colleagues. How much of the time do you spend discussing what went awry versus what went well? When you examine the proportion of time people spend focusing on the negative versus positive, you will recognize that significantly more time is spent on the negative. What do you think would happen if you spent the majority of your time focusing on the positive? Rewarding positive behavior and its impact on "being my B.E.S.T" was another key finding from my third grade experience. Let us return to my story and focus on the value of rewarding positive behavior.

~

My Story

I loved my celebrations. This one was especially wonderful because it was about my "A" on my arithmetic test. Whenever I did something good, no matter what it was, my mother would create a celebration. It was her way of showing me that she was proud of me.

Regardless of whether the celebration was between the two of us, included my dad, or involved others, my mother always knew just what to do to make me feel special. She would make sure that the dinner featured all of my favorites. Sometimes we had shrimp and fish; other times we had chicken. Sometimes we had potato salad, green beans; other times we had macaroni and cheese with collard greens. We always had a tossed salad with her special sauce. I could also count on having my favorite pound cake with her special chocolate icing. Sometimes my mother would surprise me with something special, like a scrapbook that I could use to remember my summer vacation. Usually, it was a book that could be added to my *Cherry Ames Nurse* or *Honey Bunch* collections. I loved to read both of these series. Other times, it would be something unusual but useful. My dad made me feel special too. He would bring me my favorite candy or a toy. On rare occasions, he gave me money; and when he did, he expected me to save it.

There was a knock at the door. It sprang open, and there was my big brother with more poster board and stars. "What's that for?" I inquired. "Well, the last time I checked, your scoreboard was filled with stars. I thought you might need a new one since you are starting a new reporting period." My eyes twinkled because that was just what I needed to keep track of how well I was doing with my answering questions in class, completing homework, making a "B" or better on quizzes and tests. I loved stars and was delighted that my big brother was so thoughtful. We decided to make the scoreboard while we waited on my dad to get home. After we completed the scoreboard, we hung it over my desk again so that it could be easily seen by me. As we hung the scoreboard, I boasted that soon it would be filled with even more stars than the last one.

Just as we were about to put away our materials, my dad arrived home. When I looked up, there he was with arms outstretched. "Let me give you a big hug for doing such a good job on your arithmetic test. Your mother called and told me the good news." His hugs were special to me; after all, I was a daddy's girl. Then he reached in his pocket and pulled out a five-dollar bill. My eyes really danced then; getting money from my dad was really special to me. He didn't just give it to me when I did something good. As he gave me the money, he said, "You have worked so hard over the past few weeks, and that hard work has paid off." Now I knew "working hard" was important to my dad and that was why he gave me the money. As soon as the money was in my hand, I replied, "So if I work even harder next reporting period and make an 'A,' will I get even more money?" Everyone laughed. They knew I would push the envelope. As we assembled at the table for dinner, my mother started the celebration by using her favorite line that meant everything to me, "I am so proud of Patricia." She continued, "Tonight we are celebrating her 'A' in arithmetic and the fact that she is working on being her best." She winked and smiled lovingly at me. It was our secret. There was still more for me to do to be my best. What my mother didn't know was that my goal for the next celebration was for her to say "We are celebrating Patricia being her best!"

~

At My B.E.S.T. Activity

Based upon my story, answer the following questions.

1. What rewards did I receive?

2. How did the rewards impact me "being my B.E.S.T."?

3. What did my parents do to make sure that I understood the purpose of the reward?

4. How did my big brother involve me in the reward's process?

5. How did the timing of the rewards impact me "being my B.E.S.T."?

Go to www.OmgGetsresults.com to compare your answers to mine.

Rewards come in two forms. They can be either tangible (material) or intangible (nonmaterial). In my story, both forms were provided. There were more intangible rewards than tangible. The intangible rewards appeared to work as well as the tangible because they were things that were important to me—things I valued. For example, the celebrations always had my favorite foods. Stars, which I liked, were used to track my performance. Since I was a daddy's girl, hugs from him were special. The tangible rewards were equally as meaningful. The book was important because it was one that was a part of a series that I enjoyed reading. The money had value because it was something my dad did not freely give. So when it was given, it was seen as significant.

Something to Think About . . .

1. What tangible rewards do you prefer?
2. What intangible rewards are important to you?
3. How do you respond when you get a reward that is not meaningful to you?

Rewarding positive behavior has an important benefit. The individual rewarded is motivated to continue exhibiting the positive behavior. It is easier to repeat a behavior than it is to change a behavior. So focusing me on answering questions in class versus focusing me on "stopping crying" is easier. The more I answered questions and participated in class, the less likely I was to cry. In fact, by focusing on the positive, my classroom behavior became more positive and the negative behavior subsided.

Something to Think About . . .

1. Think about a behavior you want to change. How might focusing on the positive be more beneficial than the negative?

2. Which is easier for you?
   - Remember to keep doing something
   - Remember to stop doing something

Making rewards visible is valuable because the rewards become a reminder of the behavior that you want to see repeated. In my story, the scoreboard was hung over my desk so that I could see the stars. The stars were daily visual reminders of the behaviors that my big brother wanted me to continue—asking questions in class, completing my homework, etc. When you can visually see a reward, it becomes a visual reminder of your B.E.S.T.

Something to Think About . . .

1. What visible reminders do you have of positive behaviors that you want to continue?
2. Where are some places that you have placed rewards so that you can be reminded of behaviors that you want to continue?

Both my parents consistently made it clear to be what behaviors they were recognizing. They stated the behavior as they gave me the reward. My dad told me he was rewarding "my hard work." My mother was rewarding "my 'A' in arithmetic and my working toward being my best." Knowing what the reward was directed toward is important because it does not leave it up to the person receiving the reward to misinterpret and subsequently not repeat the appropriate behavior.

As you focus on "being your B.E.S.T.," be sure to create your B.E.S.T. rewards. Engage your B.E.S.T. buddy and others in assisting you with your reward system. You want to reward yourself when your actions are aligned with your words, consistent with your plan, maintain balance between your mind, body, and spirit. Select rewards that have meaning to you so that they will motivate and reinforce you to continue your actions that will result in you "being your B.E.S.T." *Remember, only your B.E.S.T. is good enough!*

Points to Remember

- **Intangible rewards can be as beneficial as tangible if they are of value to the individual being rewarded.** What is more important than whether the reward is material or nonmaterial is how meaningful it is to the person being rewarded.

- **Negative behavior diminishes as positive behavior increases.** By focusing on positive behavior, you will ultimately eliminate the negative behavior that you don't desire.

- **Be clear about what behavior you are rewarding.** Providing specific feedback that identifies the positive behavior helps the person who is receiving the reward to know exactly what behavior should be repeated to receive the reward again.

- **Give rewards that have meaning to the individuals who will receive them.** If you are going to engage people in your life space in your rewards system, make sure you tell them what rewards are meaningful to you.

What will you do with this information to "be your B.E.S.T."?

Epilogue

Be Your B.E.S.T. is the first of a series of B.E.S.T. books that are designed to assist you in obtaining your desired results. The next book to be published will become your guide to discoveries that will lead you to *Give Your B.E.S.T.*

When you give your best, you get your best!

Coming soon is the B.E.S.T. series created for children, ages eight to twelve. It is my intention through this series to share important messages about "being your best" that were imparted to me at an early age. This series is designed to enlighten children about how to:

- Be their B.E.S.T
- Prepare for everything
- Make informed choices
- Turn lemons into lemonade
- Grab hold to opportunities

Simply speaking, the B.E.S.T. is yet to come!

Index

G

goals, 25-26, 58-59, 88-94, 96-97
  characteristics of, 89
  long-term, 93-94
  short-term, 93-94

I

information, 21-25, 27-37, 54, 66-69,
    75-77
intangible reward, 106-7
interpretation, 67-72
  definition of, 68
  sample of, 70

L

law of attraction, 97
Little Gypsy Tearoom, 39
location, 34, 36, 40-44, 46-47, 49-50,
    53

M

meaning, 49, 53, 67-68, 75-76, 109.
    See also interpretation
measurement, 22-23, 25, 67, 76-80,
    97
  basics of, 25-30
  making a habit of, 34-36
  skills of, 30-34
  See also individual skills

O

Obama, Barack, 55
obesity, 28
observation, 30-31
observation buddy, 61
osteoarthritis, 27-28

P

pedometers, 29, 79
people, 40-45, 47-50, 52-53, 55-58,
    60. *See also* context
personal roadmap. *See* BEST plan
plan, 86
  acting on, 94-97
  desired outcomes of, 86-88
  execution of, 98
  goals for, 89-94
    See also goals
  key areas of, 88
  preparations for, 98-100
  resources for, 97
preparation, 58-60, 65, 97-99

Q

questions, 33-34
  closed, 33-35
  open, 33-34, 46, 48